Praise for *Find Your*

"Drawing on years of research, Marcus l... vidual identify her strengths. It guides th... ...engins to work in order to play to her best advantage in all aspects of life. *Find Your Strongest Life* is an excellent resource not only for women, but for any executive who manages, advocates, or guides the development of women."

—**Camille Mirshokrai**, Director of Leadership Development, Accenture

"Marcus Buckingham is amazingly in touch with what women need to set ourselves up to win in life and work. In *Find Your Strongest Life*, he's developed a powerful program to identify and leverage your true strengths in the midst of the pressure of trying to have it all. Read this book and you will know all the secrets of living a strong life, and you will learn to walk confidently toward the unique and fulfilling life waiting for you—the life in which you win."

—**Lori Goler**, Head of HR, Facebook

"In this groundbreaking book, Marcus exposes the powerful myths that unduly complicate the lives of women, smashes the wrong assumptions that steer us away from happiness and success, and unveils a refreshingly insightful and powerfully simple program to get us the lives we deserve. As a woman, wife, businesswoman, mother, daughter, friend—I've never encountered such an inspired message that grasps all the roles we play and offers a path to a truly strong, authentic, and fulfilling life. I'll be coming back to this book for years!"

—**Susan Gambardella**, Region Vice-President, Coca Cola North America

"What Marcus has to say about the myth of balance is worth the price of admission. For so long I've strived for "balance" because I thought that's what everyone needed from me. Now I know my strongest life is something altogether different. This book is full of insight and tips that cut against the grain of what you thought to be true. This is a book about sustainable happiness and true success. You must read *Find Your Strongest Life*! It will change your life!"

—**Monna Nevils**, Sr. Vice President, Talent Systems, Jones Lang LaSalle

"Most of us probably have what it takes to be successful. What most people *don't* have is the foggiest idea of how to tap into those strengths and realize that success. Marcus Buckingham's common sense guidance is useful for anyone who believes there is something more (and better!) in store for them."

—**Deborah Norville**, Anchor, *Inside Edition* and Author, *The Power of Respect*

Marcus gets it! I'm the kind of woman who is always looking for new ways to live healthier and happier, and Marcus has a direct line to the heart and mind of women. This is an insightful and empowering message—you must read *Find Your Strongest Life*.

—**Robin McGraw**, #1 *New York Times* Best-Selling Author

FIND YOUR STRONGEST LIFE

WHAT THE HAPPIEST AND MOST SUCCESSFUL WOMEN DO DIFFERENTLY

MARCUS BUCKINGHAM

THOMAS NELSON
Since 1798

NASHVILLE   DALLAS   MEXICO CITY   RIO DE JANEIRO   BEIJING

Published in Nashville, Tennessee, by Thomas Nelson. Thomas Nelson is a registered trademark of Thomas Nelson, Inc.

Thomas Nelson, Inc. titles may be purchased in bulk for educational, business, fund-raising, or sales promotional use. For information, please e-mail SpecialMarkets@ThomasNelson.com.

Names, dates, places, and other identifying details have been changed to protect the identities of those mentioned.

ISBN: 978-1-4002-8078-0 (IE)

Library of Congress Cataloging-in-Publication Data

Buckingham, Marcus.
  Find your strongest life : what the happiest and most successful women
do differently / Marcus Buckingham.
      p. cm.
  Includes bibliographical references.
  ISBN 978-1-4002-0236-2
  1. Women—Psychology. 2. Self-actualization (Psychology) 3. Success.
I. Title.
  HQ1206.B7973 2009
  155.3'33—dc22   2009019560

Printed in the United States of America

09 10 11 12 13 RRD 9 8 7 6 5 4 3 2 1

To Jo, Pippa, Lilia and Jane,
the women who shape my life

CONTENTS

- Deficit Attention Disorder
- The Power of Positive Attention
- Jack's Statue

PART 3—STRONG LIFE TACTICS

TEN MYTHS ABOUT THE LIVES OF WOMEN

1. **As a result of having better education, better jobs, and better pay, women today are happier and more fulfilled than they were forty years ago.** Actually, the opposite is true. Surveys of more than 1.3 million men and women reveal that women today are less happy relative to where they were forty years ago, and relative to men.

2. **Women become more engaged and fulfilled as they get older.** No, men do. According to a forty-year study of forty-six thousand men and women, women begin their lives more satisfied than men and then gradually become less satisfied with every aspect of their lives—marriage, finances, things they own, even family.

3. **At work, women are relegated to lower-level roles.** Actually a higher percentage of women (37 percent) hold managerial or supervisory positions as compared to men (31 percent).

4. **Most men think that men should be the primary breadwinner and women should be the primary caretaker of home and family.** Most men used to think this—74 percent of men agreed with this statement in 1977. Today, however, that number has fallen to only

42 percent—which happens to be almost exactly the same as the percentage of women who agree with it (39 percent.) Your opinion of which roles are most appropriate for men and women to play is not now determined by your sex.

5. **Women would prefer to work for other women.** Most wouldn't. In fact, almost twice as many women want to work for men rather than women; 40 percent compared to 26 percent, with the remainder saying they wouldn't care one way or the other.

6. **If women had more free time, they would feel less stressed.** It doesn't appear so. According to a twenty-five-year study, each extra hour of free time doubles a man's feelings of relaxation, but does nothing for a woman's.

7. **Having children makes women happier.** Not necessarily. It turns out that kids are a bundle of stress. All studies linking stress and satisfaction with motherhood reveal the same finding: married mothers are always more stressed and less happy than married women with no kids. (I know, you love your kids, but this finding has been repeated so many times, in so many countries, there's no escaping it.)

8. **Kids want more time with their working mothers.** Not according to the kids. Most mothers think they do, but when one thousand third through twelfth graders were

asked what they wanted from their mom, only 10 percent said "more time." Their most common request (34 percent): "I want my mom to be less stressed and tired."

9. **Women are good at multitasking, and it helps them get everything done.** Two no's on this one. First, women are no better than men at multitasking. (These are tests in a lab, mind you, not tests in your home.) Second, research shows that your IQ drops ten points when you try to do two tasks at the same time—multitasking is just a nice way of saying "divided attention."

10. **Women do more housework per week than men.** Okay, this one's true. (Seventeen hours for women. Thirteen hours for men.)

INTRODUCTION

The Opposite of Juggling

Not Throwing, but Catching

Recently, my wife, Jane, attended a forum in California organized by the governor's wife, Maria Shriver. The Women's Conference, as it was called, brought together thousands of the most influential and accomplished women in the world, among them feminist icon Gloria Steinem. After her talk, a woman asked Ms. Steinem if she could explain what she meant by "You can have it all" when, the woman continued, "We clearly can't have it all."

The gist of Ms. Steinem's reply was that she'd been misunderstood. She never said, "You can have it all." What she said was that she didn't think men, or society at large, should define women's choices. Women should be able to make any choice they wanted. But, according to Gloria Steinem herself, she never said, "You can have it all."

Jane told me this story over dinner that night. Jane is a remarkable woman. She wrote her first book at sixteen, and parlayed that success into a multimillion-dollar company with offices in New York and Los Angeles. She's an author and television presenter, a fantastic mother, and everything I could ever want in a wife. But she's also someone who will freely admit that she may have pushed too hard in trying to have it all. She is the kind of mother who is determined to pick up our children, Jack and Lilia, from school every afternoon even if it means juggling calls and keeping one eye on her BlackBerry. When she's invited to appear on *Good Morning America* or the *Today* show in New York, she'll insist on taking the red-eye from our home in Los Angeles so she won't miss Jack's pitching or Lilia's ballet practice. And after the show, she'll take the earliest plane back to the office. As a woman who has built a happy and loving family while simultaneously thriving as an entrepreneur, Jane seems to have succeeded in living up to everyone's ideal.

Yet Jane knows full well that there is a price to be paid for trying to have it all. She knows how hard it is to let go of work when she's with the kids, and to let go of the kids when she's hard at work. She knows she sometimes runs on too little sleep. She has had migraines that withstood everything she hit them with. And she even, on a couple of scary occasions, has fainted during presentations.

So, the way I see it, on hearing Ms. Steinem's comment, "I never said women could have it all," Jane would have been entirely within her rights to throw up her hands in righteous frustration and say, "Thanks, Gloria. Thanks very much. Couldn't you have told us this twenty years ago? It would have made my life a heck of a lot easier."

But she didn't. Righteous frustration is not Jane's style. Instead, she just looked at me across the dining table and smiled, "Does that mean my life's a typo?"

Jane's joking aside, is Gloria Steinem right? Is it impossible for women to "have it all"? On the surface, it would seem so. Trying to be all things to all people all of the time is a fool's game that will, in the end, drain mind, body, and spirit.

But dig a little deeper and you have to ask yourself, "What's the alternative?" If Jane tells herself that she can't have it all, then what's she left with? Three-quarters of a life? Half a life? Less than half? An approach to life that begins with the question, "Which parts of myself must I cut out?" inevitably leads to a laundry list of unhealthy emotions: panic that you can't cut out enough, confusion over which parts to cut out, fear that you've cut out the wrong parts, guilt about that fear, and resentment about all of it.

Jane shouldn't be asking herself, "Which parts of myself should I cut out?" Nor should you. It's the wrong question.

The right question is, "What do I mean by 'having it all'?" Because if "having it all" means drawing enough strength from life to feel fulfilled, loved, successful, and in control, then that is something every single one of us should aim for and every single one of us can attain.

"Having it all" doesn't mean having everything, all at once, all the time. "Having it all" means taking yourself seriously. It means knowing yourself well enough to find your purpose in life. It means knowing what needs to change when you sense that you've lost that purpose. It means having the faith to believe that change is possible and having the courage to make those changes. It means drawing strength from the relationships in your life, and, if there's no strength to be drawn, knowing when to cut those relationships out of your life.

It means mastering the skill of using life to fill you up. That is all you can do, and it is everything you need to do.

The conventional image of a successful woman today is that she's a virtuoso juggler, somehow moving fast enough to keep all the many aspects of her busy life in the air at the same time. Conventional it may be, but it's also quite sad. The core skill of juggling is throwing, not catching. To keep every object in the air, you have to get rid of each one as quickly as possible, barely allowing it to register on your fingertips before you toss it up and away, preparing for the next object to throw.

A strong life is the opposite of juggling. Juggling requires you to keep everything at bay, up in the air, away from you. The secret to living a strong life lies in knowing how to draw a few things in toward you. It asks you to be discriminating, selective, intentional. You can find energizing moments in each aspect of your life, but to do so you must learn how to catch them, hold on to them, feel the pull of their weight, and allow yourself to follow where they lead.

The aim of this book is to teach you this life skill.

This book will show you how to start your life strong and then, more importantly, how to get stronger as you get older. It will help you set a direction for your life without fearing that you've chosen the wrong one. It will reveal how to handle all the responsibilities on your shoulders without feeling spasms of guilt that you aren't doing enough, or that what you're doing you're doing wrong. It will guide you toward building fulfilling relationships with your boss, your coworkers, your spouse, and your kids without letting resentment of what they are demanding *from* you, or what they are not doing *for* you, slip in.

Of course, this book won't answer all your questions nor will it solve all your problems, but it will show you how you can use life to strengthen you, rather than break you down. It will show you how to find your strongest life.

You'll begin by taking a test, the Strong Life test, that measures you on nine life roles: Advisor, Caretaker, Creator, Equalizer, Influencer, Motivator, Pioneer, Teacher, and Weaver. More than likely, your life calls on you to play all nine roles some of the time, but, even so, you are not a blank slate—your personality doesn't shift and morph according to the demands of every unique situation. Instead, as we all do, you have some *consistent* patterns of thinking, feeling, and behaving, patterns that are distinctive and that remain stable across time and situations. These patterns come together in a Lead Role, a role you return to time and again, a role that you and your closest family and friends recognize as the core of who you are. It is the role in which, today, you feel most authentic, in control, and effective. Here, in this role, you are versatile and resilient and courageous. Here, you learn fast and easily, and are always hungry to learn more. Here is the source of your genius, at home and at work.

Next, you'll learn how to accept your Lead Role and build your life around it. This doesn't mean you have to abandon the grand dreams you have for your life—on the contrary, more often than not acceptance is the necessary precondition for discovering exactly *how* you can live out these dreams. Acceptance does require a clear head, though. You are surrounded by so many different people, each with their own expectations of you, each placing their demands on you, each competing for your attention. You need the right mindset to cut through the clamor of these competing voices, and take a stand for who you really are.

Finally, you'll learn how to intentionally imbalance your life. So often you are told to strive for balance. But balance is the wrong target—it is almost impossible to achieve and unfulfilling when you do. Study the happiest and most successful women and you realize that they ignore balance, and strive for fullness instead. They deliberately tilt their world toward those few moments that genuinely fill them up. This isn't self-centeredness. It is the strong life practice that gives them the strength they need to provide for all those who rely on them.

To help you put this practice to work in your own life, you'll end the book with a series of Strong Life tactics. Here you'll get down to brass tacks and learn how you can use this practice to find you're your strongest career, to strengthen your relationships, to raise strong kids, and to build a stronger future for yourself. I arranged it in a simple question-and-answer format so you can pick which areas you want to dive into more deeply and find the practical tips you need to take control of your life.

However, it's impossible to begin any journey unless you know where you're starting from, so, before you launch into the Strong Life test, it's worth taking time to pinpoint where you are today. By which I mean, are you happy? Are you fulfilled? Are you clear about which direction your life should take? Do you know what success would look like and feel like if you were lucky enough to find it?

If you are a woman, the chances of you answering 'yes' to these questions are lower today than forty years ago, and lower than if you were a man. After forty years of research into men's and women's happiness, the evidence reveals that, though both men and women can suffer under life's pressures and uncertainties, women seem to be suffering more. To discover why, and learn what you can do to increase your happiness and success, we're going to head to Chicago and a frigid Fall morning outside the refurbished hockey rink Harpo productions now calls home.

PART 1

SOMETHING'S GOT TO GIVE

ONE WORKSHOP, ONE SHOW, ONE HUNDRED THOUSAND QUESTIONS

What do all women want to know?

> To live is so startling it leaves little
> time for anything else.
>
> —EMILY DICKINSON (1830–1886), American poet

'm the odd man out, standing on a Chicago street corner staring at a long line of people snaking down the block. It's early and it's cold, the wind tearing off the lake and through my hopeless cotton coat. I was in Puerto Vallarta the day before, squeezing in a quick vacation with my wife and kids, and the coat had been a waste of space in my suitcase, as bulky and unnecessary as a snowsuit. Today, I'm wishing I'd packed the snowsuit.

I go through the motions of turning up my flimsy collar against the wind and keep staring at the line of people.

I hadn't realized it would be like this, that people would be so excited, showing up hours before the show, laughing with delight, and bobbing about on the balls of their feet. It reminds me of a line outside a rock concert. A line of women, all ages and races, daughters and mothers, sisters together, dressed to the nines, blown-out hair, sleek skirts and shiny pumps, all waiting to be part of the show, their show, the *Oprah Winfrey Show*.

I'm here to be part of the show too—more specifically, I'm here to tape a three-hour workshop titled "Career Intervention." The producers at the *Oprah Winfrey Show* recently learned that many of their viewers don't watch the show live; they record it. This means that most of these viewers must be working during the day and then coming home and watching their favorite shows in the evening. And if most of them are working, so the producers' thinking went, then they will want to know how to find fulfilling work, exciting work, work they're passionate about. So the producers put out a call through Oprah.com for any unhappy working women—not, it turns out, a rare breed. They sifted through the avalanche of responses, selected a short list of one hundred talented but unfulfilled women, interviewed those one hundred, narrowed the list to thirty, and invited them to a workshop with Oprah herself. And then they called me.

This is my expertise. I'm a strength strategist. I help companies and individuals identify their strengths and devise the right strategies to put those strengths to work. I've been doing this for twenty years now, ever since I up and left my home in the UK and joined the Gallup Organization.

During my time at Gallup I learned the art and the science of designing questions to measure a person's unique strengths. And by "strengths" I don't mean the ability to play the violin or paint a portrait or run the hundred meters in less than ten seconds. Instead, I mean abilities like empathy, patience, assertiveness, or courage. If you want to know whether a person is truly courageous, what questions would you ask? Would you ask, "Are you ever aggressive and challenge people more than you should?" Or how about, "Tell me about a time when you overcame resistance to your ideas?" Or maybe something really simple: "On a scale of 1 to 10 with 10 high, how courageous are you?" Or maybe all of the above.

This sort of stuff is riveting to me. That you can sort through all the possible "courage" questions and identify the most powerful ones, and that you can do the same for questions to predict a person's talent to be charming, responsible, or empathetic, and that you can ask the questions in such a way that the person will reveal herself even when she knows that this is precisely what you are trying to get her to do—all of this is, for me, well, gobsmacking. It's awesome and exciting and mystifying and cool, all at once.

Driven by this fascination with personal strengths, I've written three books on how you can identify and apply your own, the first titled *Now, Discover Your Strengths*, its follow-up *Go Put Your Strengths to Work*, and a DVD/book tool kit called *The Truth about You*.[1]

I've even founded my own company—TMBC—to help leaders and managers capitalize on the strengths of their people. So many of us wander through life unaware of what our true strengths are, or, though we might know what they are, we struggle to play to our strengths at home or at work. In fact, in polls asking, "What percentage of a typical day do you get to play your strengths?" only 14 percent of us say "Most of the time."

My life's mission is to increase this number. This mission has taken different forms at different times in my career—I've written books, given speeches, produced films, coached executives, and consulted with large organizations—but the mission itself has remained constant. And I have no doubt it will remain constant for the rest of my working life. It's not an intellectual thing—though devising the questions and figuring out the strength strategies is intellectual. But the mission itself is instinctive; it's what my heart seeks out when I reach for purpose and what my mind naturally returns to when all else is quiet.

I see it in my visceral fascination with why two people of the same gender and race and age can be so different in terms of how well they remember names or how impatient they are or how organized. I feel it in my need to involve myself in someone else's life and tell her what she should do to capitalize on her unique gifts. I wouldn't necessarily call myself an altruistic person in all aspects of my life—I'm neither a natural caregiver nor a warm shoulder to cry on—but when it comes to advising someone on how to make the most of herself, I just can't stop myself. I dive in, dig around, prod, push, and cajole. It's an irresistible compulsion, telling me, *Each person is born different. You must do everything in your power to help her capitalize on this difference.*

I imagine that somewhere, deep inside one of my chromosomes, you would find this mission written in the language of DNA code. I choose to write it this way:

My mission is to help each person identify her strengths, take them seriously, and offer them to the world.

I began my career focusing this mission in the world of work, not least because the most successful working people are so effective at it. However, over the last twenty years, it's become increasingly clear to me that I needed to extend this strengths-based approach to life beyond work.

First, simply because the working world led me there. When I am coaching senior executives on how to leverage their own strengths, or how to build an entire strengths-based organization, inevitably the conversation broadens beyond the competencies one needs to get a job done. In our knowledge/service economy, where the value of most jobs now lies in the employee's talents and relationships, organizations need to understand and appreciate the full authenticity of each human being that works for them, not just to keep employees engaged, but, more importantly, to tap into each person's creativity, innovation, and insights. The worlds of work and home and friends and hobbies and special interests are now so interwoven, both technologically and practically, that all high performing organizations must reach beyond the workplace and address the whole person.

And second, I'm reaching beyond the working world because a growing body of evidence reveals that finding and applying your strengths is the key to living a happy and successful life. The young discipline of Positive Psychology has already yielded healthy disagreements about the causes of happiness—is it driven by good health, or companionship, or purchasing power, or a match between what you want and what you actually get—, about whether your level of happiness is changeable—some assert that we each have our own happiness 'set-point' and that nothing, no matter how tragic or wonderful, can move the dial, while others take a less fatalistic view—, and even about whether total happiness is the right goal—some recent research suggests that people who rate themselves 8 or 9 on a happiness scale wind up being more successful than people who give themselves a full 10 out of 10.

However, when it comes to making people both happy and

effective, all agree—from the 'psychologists' such Albert Bandura, Mihaly Csikszentmihalyi, and Martin Seligman to the 'economists' such as Richard Easterlin and the Nobel prize winning Daniel Kahneman—about the awesome power of self-efficacy. Self-efficacy is not merely a general sense of self-esteem, of being a worthy person. Rather it is a feeling tied to a specific task, or activity, or situation. You feel it when you assess a specific task or activity or situation and you know, you just know, that you are in control—that you have what it takes to tackle the task, to perform the activity, to be powerful within the situation. This is not to say that you feel you have complete mastery. On the contrary, you are aware that you still have additional skills to learn. It's more that, for this specific task, for this specific activity, within this specific situation, you are thrilled by this need to learn more, to refine your technique, to experiment, to get better. Self-efficacy, then, is you at your most assured, engaged, wise and yet still inquisitive. It's the feeling you get when you are in your strengths-zone. And whether the research is conducted inside the workplace or outside, at school or at home, with students or with adults, this strength-zone feeling is always highly correlated to both happiness and effectiveness.

Spurred by this linking of strengths to happiness and effectiveness in all aspects of life, I've found myself sitting down to begin writing this "strong-life" book many times over the last twenty years. But other projects always seemed to rise up and pull my attention elsewhere. And then something happened in Chicago—an overwhelming response, an unexpected outpouring of questions—and I knew instinctively that I had to put everything else aside and write it right then.

Outside Harpo Studios the doors opened, and in we all marched,

I to the stage, the well-dressed line of women to their seats in the studio—some to watch a taping of an Oprah show, some to participate in our workshop—and then, after Oprah made the introductions, we did the workshop together: thirty talented but unfulfilled women searching for direction and purpose, one monumentally successful media executive sitting in the front row, and me.

What was supposed to happen next was this: my coaches and I were supposed to counsel each of the participants over the next few months, helping them rediscover the passion in their work or to take action to find other work, talking them through the beliefs, the people, and the obstacles that were holding them back. Then, after following the participants for six months, we were to come back together and see the changes they'd made. And we'd capture it all—the before, the journey, the after—in one hour-long show.

Indeed, this is what happened. It was a good show. I enjoyed it, Oprah seemed to enjoy it also, and, most important, the women in the workshop made significant and positive changes in their lives. And if this had been all that happened, it would have been plenty—thirty women, whose lives were stuck, had become unstuck and were now striding forward again.

But this isn't all that happened. In the weeks following the show, more than one and a half million people logged on to Oprah.com and downloaded the three-hour workshop. And then the message boards lit up like an Olympic fireworks display. More than a hundred thousand (mostly) women posted messages online, some craving help, others offering support and advice.

Here's Alijay1030, a wife and mother who is terrified of making the wrong decision:

I am scared to leave a profession that provides our family with good benefits and a paycheck that allows us to live a comfortable life while still being able to save for college, retirement, etc. Still, I ask myself if I'm "living my best life," and the answer is a resounding no. I need more. I need a purpose. I need to feel passionate about what I do. Deep down inside I know that I need to do something, I just don't know what that something is. Where do I start? I have been doing a job that I hate for so long, I have lost touch with myself. I have forgotten what I'm good at and what I enjoy doing. What do you do when you feel completely lost?

Here's Kelly, a teacher:

I should be grateful for what I have. I'm paid very handsomely for what I do, receive a great benefits package, and get the summers off. But I am tormented about my future. I know I just have to leave my job, but to do what? A faith in doing what you love is theoretically wonderful, but what if you don't know what to do? And then when you find the answer, how do you find the courage to go for it?

Here's Karlene:

If my strengths are in areas that I'm unqualified in and that will likely not pay well anyway, should I just forget it and work in an area that doesn't complement me?

Teresa asked the same thing:

What do you suggest as a place to start to those of us who need time to get into our new career but are without a current source of income and may not have that needed time? Do we trudge through taking another job in our current industry in the meantime?

Then there was Kaykel, a forty-eight-year-old flight attendant, who asked:

Can you help me not be afraid of change and help me find and follow my passion? The career was great for a long time, but I have outgrown the job and have other desires at this stage. I have a bachelor's degree from 1982, but where will that get me today?

Liz was at a different stage in life than Kaykel, but she felt the same fear:

I have been reading through many of the posts and doing a lot of soul searching myself after taking Marcus's course, and I have finally admitted to myself that I need to make a change. Now the hard part, convincing my husband and family that it is the right thing to do for all of us. I do have a great job, with a great paycheck, and great flexibility—but that I am finding is not enough. The job satisfaction is 0. Also I am not moving out of my industry, but I am methodically planning a shift of how I can use my strengths in that industry that will require leaving my secure job (set paycheck, benefits) for a less secure (commission

*based) income. Admittedly I am scared—what if I fail? What if
things don't work out? My children are still very young—should
I wait? These are all the questions that I have been asking myself
and trying to overcome. Has anyone here addressed their fears
of life change, and how have you overcome it?*

And then there was Caroline, a wife and mother who turned
down a job that would have meant sacrificing time with her family,
and then questioned her decision:

*I am the mother of beautiful twin boys who are nearly five, and,
even though me and my husband do OK, of course we worry
about what will happen and if we're going to put them through
college if this economy keeps getting worse. Now I don't know
if I've done the right thing. . . . I work in the services industry and was recently offered a position that would have given
me more money in my pocket and the chance to rise higher in
the company and more quickly. And I said no. I would like to
have the money to save for the boys but the extra hours I would
have worked would have meant me seeing them much less. And
I would have not been at home two nights a week to put them to
bed. My husband is good around the house, no real complaints
there, but I definitely do the lion's share of the work and I think
my boys like having me there. Also, I don't want to miss out on
these precious years. What do people think? We're always told
to put our priorities first and I'm doing that, but I would have
been using my strengths with my promotion and I would have
earned more, too. I just don't know if I'm totally cut out for*

being a rat in the rat race. Was I being lazy and selfish not taking the new job? Has anyone else had these concerns?

And then, of course, this one from Kelly21:

How do other women get everything done that needs to be done in the day without sacrificing their family and/or work relationships and their sense of self? Is it unrealistic to believe we can do it all?

And finally, and most poignantly, here's Vanessa:

I'm dying at work. I'm a sales rep for a drug company putting in my hours until my husband finishes his residency. I know on one level I'm doing right for my daughter, for my husband. But am I? Am I really? What kind of message am I sending to my daughter? That one day, honey, you'll grow up to be like Mommy: someone who leaves the ones she loves to go out and do a job she hates. How crazy is that!?

These questions might start with work, but they quickly bleed out beyond the working world. They deal with direction, purpose, passion, the handling of kids, work and family, the courage to make a change, the difficulty of talking it through with your family, the struggle to land on the correct definition of success. How do I tackle change without fear? When is the right time to risk a big change? When should I be selfish and put myself first, or is that even selfish? How can I be sensible and grounded and financially secure without abandoning my passion? How do I excel at being a mother, employee, and wife without losing myself in the process?

These challenges center on one all-encompassing question: how do I live a strong, fulfilling life?

You recognize these challenges, don't you? Each woman draws from the specifics of her own life, but these challenges are likely familiar to you. Whether you work and raise your kids, or stay at home and raise your kids, whether you are just starting out or are well into your career, whether you are on the right track but feel too stressed, or whether you sense you are far off track and feel completely lost, these challenges are your challenges.

In saying this, I don't want to be presumptuous—you may be one of those people who always feels focused and successful, with plenty of energy and time, and what few doubts you have are quickly drowned out by the many moments of real fulfillment. If you are, well done to you—you've succeeded in shaping life to your design.

But most women haven't. Most women struggle with the same challenges that appeared on the Oprah.com message boards. In fact, when you look closely at the data relating to women's happiness and well-being, you discover a bizarre paradox: Over the last forty years women have secured for themselves greater opportunity, greater achievement, greater influence, and more money. But over the same time period, they have become less happy, more anxious, and more stressed; and, in ever-increasing numbers, they are medicating themselves for it.

THE FEMALE PARADOX

What trap has life set?

Because the idea is, in the long run, that women's liberation will be men's liberation, too.

—GLORIA STEINEM (b.1934), author and activist

I magine it is 1969 and we're in a thriving American city. Let's choose Detroit. The sixties were good to the Motor City, and the future would have looked as bright as new chrome. Now, imagine stopping a working woman on Detroit's Woodward Avenue, perhaps a young bank clerk, and asking if she would cast her mind forward, decades into the future. Not to picture the flying cars and space-themed restaurants that always seem to pop up in visions of the future, but to think about the role of women at work, in business, in government, in life. What do you think she would have said?

The year 1969 was an intense, rousing time for women in America. Betty Friedan had published *The Feminine Mystique* a few years earlier and had founded the National Organization for Women in 1966. And Gloria Steinem, her more controversial compatriot, had just published the essay "After Black Power: Women's Liberation" in

New York Magazine that launched the modern women's movement, calling for meaningful work, equal pay, and the goal for all women to be freed from the role of only "servicing men and their children."

Fast-forward forty years: no matter how optimistic the guesses of our "woman-on-a-Detroit-street," I bet they wouldn't have outstripped what's actually happened.

I doubt she would have guessed that by the early twenty-first century, women would be running the governments of countries as powerful and widespread as Germany and Ireland, Bangladesh and New Zealand, Chile, Mozambique, and Jamaica. Or that the wife of one U.S. president would spend months in 2008 as the national favorite to become president herself and, failing in that quest, would become an outspoken secretary of state, or that the speaker of the house would be a woman. Or that John McCain, the 2008 Republican candidate for president, would choose a moose-hunting, helicopter-riding, crowd-pleasing mother of five as his running mate because she'd stared down oil companies as governor of the tough state of Alaska.

How about education? I'm sure she would have forecast that more women would be completing high school and attending college, but do you think she'd have predicted that during the 2008 school year, 59 percent of *all* the bachelor's degrees and 61 percent of *all* the master's degrees would be earned by women, not by men?[1] Or that by 2009, four out of the eight Ivy League universities—Harvard, Brown, Penn, and Princeton—would have female presidents?

And work? Again, she probably would have bet that, in the future, more women would be working, but would she have guessed that women would be holding more management and supervisory positions than men, by a margin of 37 percent to 31 percent,[2] that in like-for-like work women who have the same amount of experience as men would be earning almost exactly what men earn, and that women's pay would actually be increasing faster than men's?[3] I doubt it.

Yet the biggest surprise would have come if you had asked her just one more question. Given all the evidence of women running corporations and universities, hospitals, media empires, branches of government, and countries, do you think women in the future will be happier?

Of course they will be happy, she would have said. With all this choice and opportunity, how could they not be?

Well, as it turns out: too easily.

Each year since 1972, the United States General Social Survey has asked men and women: "How happy are you, on a scale of 1 to 3, with 3 being very happy, and 1 being not too happy?" This survey includes a representative sample of men and women of all ages, education levels, income levels, and marital status—fifteen hundred per year for a total of almost fifty thousand individuals thus far—and so it gives us a most reliable picture of what's happened to men's and women's happiness over the last few decades.

As you can imagine, a survey this massive generates a multitude of findings, but for our purposes here are the two most important discoveries.

First, since 1972, women's overall level of happiness has dropped, both relative to where they were forty years ago, and relative to men.[4] This drop in happiness is found in women regardless of whether they have kids; how many kids they have; how much money they make;

how healthy they are; what job they hold; whether they are married, single, or divorced; how old they are; or what race they are. (The one and only exception: African-American women are now slightly happier than they were back in 1972. Although they remain less happy than African-American men)

If you are a visual learner, this is what the graph looks like[5]:

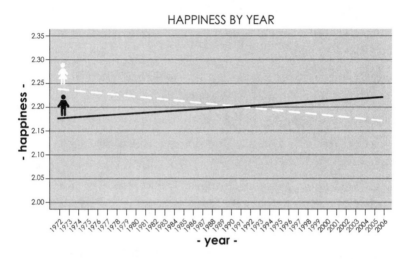

HAPPINESS BY YEAR

And, in case you're wondering, this finding is neither unique to this one study, nor is it unique to the United States. In the last couple of years, the results from six major studies of happiness have been released:

- the United States General Social Survey (46,000 people, between 1972–2007),
- the Virginia Slims Survey of American Women (26,000 people, between 1972–2000),

- the Monitoring the Future survey (430,000 U.S. twelfth graders, between 1976–2005),
- The British Household Panel Study (121,000 people, between 1991 and 2004)
- The Eurobarometer analysis (636,000 people, between 1973 and 2002, covering fifteen countries)
- The International Social Survey Program (97,462 people, between 1991 and 2001, covering thirty-five developed countries)

All told, more than 1.3 million men and women have been surveyed over the last thirty years, both here in the U.S. and in developed countries around the world. Wherever researchers have been able to collect reliable data on happiness, the finding is always the same: greater educational, political, and employment opportunities have corresponded to *decreases* in life happiness for women, as compared to men.

It feels strange to write that sentence, as though I'm mistyping or having a "backwards day," as my daughter would say. But I'm not. Though the trends in the data certainly don't suggest that all women are less happy than they were back in 1972—the trend sizes are quite small—the fact is that, across more than a million people, the trends are there, and they are going in the opposite direction than most people would have predicted.

The second discovery is this: Though women begin their lives more fulfilled than men, as they age, they gradually become less happy. Men, in contrast, get happier as they get older.[6]

Here's the graph, taken from General Social Survey data[7]:

HAPPINESS BY AGE

This creeping unhappiness can seep into all aspects of a woman's life. When the researchers asked more specific questions, such as, "How satisfied are you with your marriage?" and "How happy are you with the things you own?" and "How satisfied are you with your finances?" the pattern was always the same: women begin their lives more satisfied than men, and wind up less satisfied. Sure, the crossover points vary a little—women's happiness with their marriages sink below men's at age thirty-nine; their satisfaction with their finances dips at age forty-one; and by forty-four, they're more dissatisfied than men with stuff they own.

But overall, the trajectory is consistent, and consistently downhill. As you can see from the graph, by the time women reach age forty-seven, they are, overall, less happy with their lives than men, and the trend continues on down from there.

Of course, this doesn't mean that every individual woman becomes less happy than every individual man—we all have our own stuff going on, and man or woman, some days we're in a happy purple haze, some days we've got the blues, and some days we even succumb to the "mean reds," as Holly Golightly called them. Nor does it mean that this darkening outlook on life is necessarily going to afflict *you*. You are a unique human being, blessed with the freedom to make your own choices, and so it's completely within your power to choose a life, and a perspective on life, that becomes *more* fulfilling as you get older, not less. There'd be little point reading a book such as this if you didn't believe you had this power.

However, right now, the two trends we see in the data are real and telling:

1. Over the last few decades, women have become less happy with their lives.
2. As women get older, they get sadder.

Look around and you can easily find other research that confirms and colors these two trends. Take stress as an example. Sociologists from Ohio State University examined time diary data from two national surveys, one conducted in 1976 and the other in 1999, to see whether men's and women's experience of their "free time" had changed over twenty years.[8] Here's what they found:

> ○ *Women were much more likely to feel sometimes or always rushed in 1999 than in 1975, while men were not.* So not only are women becoming less happy decade by decade, but their minutes are becoming more stress-filled as well.

- *Each hour of free time reduces men's odds of feeling rushed by 8 percent, but each hour of free time has no similar effect for women.* So whatever is happening to women in their so-called free time is not helping them feel less stressed.
- *For women, the odds of feeling sometimes or always rushed are 2.2 times higher for married women with children than for single, childless women. The same is not true for men.* Translation: kids inhibit relaxation for women, but not for men.

Looking beyond pure survey data, the World Health Organization can track what this increase in stress does to a woman's mental health. According to their most recent analysis, depression is the second most debilitating disease for women (heart disease is first), while for men depression clocks in at number ten.[9] As a result, women choose to medicate themselves with antianxiety and antidepression medication twice as much as men do. Never one to miss an opportunity, the big pharmaceutical companies nurse this need by targeting two-thirds of all advertising of these medications explicitly toward women.

To provide texture to all this data, let's return to the Oprah.com message boards and a few of the stories behind the data:

Countess1:

Lost, but not forgotten. That's how I feel about my dreams. I've been on a personal journey for several years that included finding what I am uniquely created to do. Although I'm quite sure I know, I have no idea how to get there. I am a single mother of twin boys, and spend all my money trying to keep them in private school because we live in one of the worst school districts in our state. I'm working three jobs to make ends meet. I've been working on my dream as well, but the day job is so depleting, demoralizing, and demanding that I hardly have anything left when it's all said and done.

Schadd66:

I have been the breadwinner for the last twelve years, and I am unhappy with my job. My husband sacrificed so that I could go to school for nursing. The money has been great, but I am not happy with my job. I thought if I went back to school for my BSN and then my MSN that I would find other jobs in nursing that I would like, but that hasn't happened. I have tried numerous types of nursing including teaching nursing and working in administration, but I am not happy. I continue working in the field because I believe I owe it to my husband and children. I dread getting up and going to work every day.

Jkursenski:

After nine years at a high-profile job in the entertainment field, I was dying inside. Just as the women on the show expressed, a bit was breaking off every day. I knew it was time to end it, which I did. But now what? I've been home for a few months taking a break, but don't know where to turn from here. I went from someone who was somebody to no one in particular. . . . Where do I go from here?

Luveyduvey, a single mom, forty-eight years old, who's been a manager for her twenty-six-year career in higher education, she was recently laid off:

> *I am good at what I do and confident about my skills and abilities. My problem is that I never realized that I was relying on my work life and accomplishments to define who I am. Now that it's gone, or at least temporarily, I feel totally lost. . . . I'm tired, worn down, and done with being unappreciated and overworked.*

Reneeliz, a mom of twin five-year-olds who has just enrolled in school to become a radiology tech because the dollars are good, realized before starting school:

> *This is not me! I was always creative as a child, loved the arts and writing. Somewhere down the line I figured that those qualities wouldn't get me anywhere in life if I wasn't the best at them, so I tucked that away and forgot about it. I don't know who I am anymore and I haven't for years! I always wanted a job that I could look forward to, and right now I can't find that anywhere! I am thirty-eight years old and don't know what to do when I grow up. Help!*

"Hey," you might say. "Life's tough. Deal with it." And of course, you'd be right. Life is not designed with anyone's happiness in mind, and it has the disconcerting habit of not rewarding the good as much as we'd expect, of punishing the wicked less vigorously than we'd like, and even, on occasion, of getting the two completely mixed up.

Even so, only the most wasted of cynics would deny that something's got to give. Not only is this "tough life" significantly tougher on women than it is on men, but the advances of the last forty years were supposed to have changed things for the better. And not just for womankind, but for each individual woman. The hard-won rights, opportunities, and advantages were supposed to have netted women more than just another burdensome role to play—"you at work." They were supposed to have fostered in each woman feelings of fulfillment and happiness, and even, for the special few, the sustained thrill of living an authentic life.

This hasn't happened. Whether you're looking at the data or reading these stories or just listening to the sound of your own voice, the conclusion is hard to escape: over the last forty years or so, life has not become more fulfilling for women; it has, in every way we can measure, become more draining instead. To use Thomas Jefferson's words, though women now have the liberty to choose whichever life they'd like, they are struggling in their pursuit of a *happy* life.

WHAT TO TAKE AWAY FROM THIS CHAPTER

- **Over the last forty years, women have become less happy than they were, and less happy than men.** This pattern holds true regardless of their marital status, whether they work or raise kids or both, number of children they have, or level of education.

- **As women grow older they gradually become less satisfied with all aspects of life.** By contrast, men's satisfaction increases with age.

- **Both of these trend-lines are moving in the opposite direction from what one would have predicted given women's dramatic advances in education, employment opportunities, earning power, and societal/political influence.**

- **These trend-lines are meaningful in size.** To give you an idea of their significance, if we assume a strong link between being unhappy and being unemployed (which there is—the longer you're out of work, the more depressed you become,) the decline in women's happiness is as if women's unemployment has risen from 10% to 18%.

- **Women's daily levels of stress are higher now than they were forty years ago, and adding more free time does little to lessen these feelings of stress.**

- **Women consume twice as much anti-depression and anti-anxiety medication as men,** and as a result (or perhaps a cause of this disparity) pharmaceutical companies target these drugs toward women more aggressively than they do toward men.

- **Though each of these trends represent a 'headwind' for you,** you can take action to reverse these trends in your own life.

OF CHOICE AND MEN

What gets in the way of your happiness?

One never notices what has been done;
one can only see what remains to be done.

—MARIE CURIE (1867–1934), French scientist

What is it that has made modern life so much more stressful for women?

The causes are as many and varied as there are women alive, but running through all this diversity are two common causes, and, sadly, both of them are chronic—meaning you will never be rid of them; all you can do is learn to control them. Equally sadly, neither will be a surprise to you—most women know what's hurting them, even if they aren't sure what to do about it. Let's take a closer look at each of these causes.

Excess Choice

One explanation for what's hurting women, of course, is that the two sides of the paradox are linked. The reason women are more anxious and stressed today is *because* they now have more opportunities, more choice and therefore more 'domains' in which they have to measure up. In which case, we have a problem. Choice is supposed to be good, isn't it? Sure, it can be really difficult to juggle the demands of work and family and friends, but who would want to rewind the clock forty years back to a time when you couldn't get the education you wanted, or the job, or the promotion, or the raise?

Very few women would. (In the Virginia Slims 1999 poll, 72% of women said that "women having more choices in society today gives women more opportunities to be happy.") Most women want to have the freedom to make the choice about whether to work, and when presented with this choice, most women do indeed choose to work. You have to go all the way back to 1974 for the last year that most women preferred to stay home (60 percent). Today, when given the choice between working or staying home, only 45 percent of women choose home.[1]

And this isn't a fake choice borne out of financial necessity, as in "I have to work in order to afford our chosen lifestyle." It's a choice driven by the desire to find opportunities outside the home to express yourself and make a productive contribution. Of course, I don't know this for certain, but it's the most obvious explanation for the fact that 72 percent of women whose husbands earn between $60,000 and $120,000 still choose to work.[2] (If your husband makes more than $120,000, you're still more likely to be working than not, 54 to 46 percent.)

Of course, there is one particular group of women who have no choice but to work: single mothers. The data reveal that if you are a single mother and you don't work, you are six times more likely to live in poverty than if you do work.[3] A choice between work and poverty isn't much of a choice.

But still, most women do have a genuine choice about how to spend their waking hours, and most women want this choice. The challenge with choice, though, is that when you have one, you have to make one, and, more importantly, you have to make the right one. Whether you like it or not, the responsibility lies with you to sort through all the possible choices you could make and land on the very few you *should* make, and then, having narrowed down your options, you are supposed to make your choice with no fear, no guilt, and no lingering regret.

For a woman today this is almost impossibly hard, because the choices are so numerous and the stakes so high. Should you have a child first and then focus on your job? Should you follow your artistic dream now or wait until you've saved money in the bank? Is it better to take the job with fewer responsibilities if it means more time with your family? Should you keep your child at home or send her to day care? Work longer hours to afford a better-qualified nanny? Answer that e-mail or finish your son's puzzle? Care for your mother or take that banking job to help pay for her nurse? Stay in a job that numbs you or risk it all for one that doesn't? Risk everything for yourself or stay settled for others? The questions are endless; the answers open-ended; the consequences of making the wrong choice almost too frightening to contemplate. You may hope that being at work while your child is at day care is a sensible option—and, as the research shows, it can be—but you know you would never forgive yourself if the choice proved to be wrong.

With so many choices, how can you ever know you are making the right ones? How can you ever feel happy and secure?

According to Barry Schwartz, professor of social theory at

Swarthmore College, you can't. In his studies of the psychology of choice, he has discovered that, contrary to what we might believe, having so many choices in our lives doesn't make us happy.[4] It doesn't free us. It can paralyze us. For example, in one of many such studies, he found a negative correlation between the number of 401(k) plans offered to a firm's employees and the number of employees who actually chose a plan. In other words, the more plans the company offered, the more likely people were to choose no plan at all. They lost money because they were too overwhelmed by the excess of choice.

And why does an excess of choice paralyze us? According to Schwartz, the psychological result of too many choices is that we're always in search of an elusive perfection. We don't just want a pair of jeans. Instead, enticed by rack upon rack, shelf upon shelf, we want the perfect pair of jeans, the best flat-screen TV, the smartest nanny for our kids, the truly perfect job. Lured by the possibility of the perfect anything, we wind up devoting far too much time to the process of choosing, ruminating back and forth, and then, after we've chosen, questioning our decision. With so many options available, it becomes almost impossible to be satisfied with the one we picked.

So although some choice is clearly better than no choice, a multitude of choice isn't better than some choice. Professor Schwartz's work confirms what, I imagine, you've long suspected: it's hard to make fear-free, guilt-free, regret-free choices when you're faced with so many.

It becomes harder still when the people who know you, love you, and care about you insist on weighing in on which choice is the right one for you.

Of course you're unhappy, your mother tells you. You're working too hard, you're not spending enough time with the kids, you're not sitting down for enough meals with the family, and you sure aren't cooking those meals at home. You're not getting pregnant because you're too stressed at work or you're not spending enough time in the bedroom with your man, or both.

And if that wasn't criticism enough . . .

You're not healthy because you have no time for the gym, you're not losing weight because you eat fast food on the fly, and you're definitely not getting any younger. "I may not have had a job," she'll say as she slips the knife in, "but at least I was a great mom. And I was happy."

Your girlfriend, inevitably, thinks your mom couldn't be more wrong. Your girlfriend knows how you'd go crazy if you stayed at home with the kids. She tells you that you need to focus *more* on work, make an impression with the boss, get a pay raise, be more aggressive, stay longer than anyone else. Isn't that what women have spent fifty years fighting for, she asks? To be able to work as hard as men, earn as much as men, delegate life's dull duties to others, just like men? Go for it, she goads. If Hillary can do it, and Sarah can do it, and that woman who runs Pepsi can do it, so can you.

That path sounds hard and challenging, but she's right: you like to work. It's an important part of who you are. Perhaps you should listen to her. But then your colleague reminds you that everyone in upper management has a master's degree and you don't. So now the only way for you to move forward is to go back to college and get the education you need. Except you have a mortgage lender breathing down your neck, or a husband whose small business has been hurting recently, or a house filled with kids who don't have a clue what the magazines mean when they print that Mommy needs "me time," "alone space," and a vacation somewhere where the sun is hot and soccer practice isn't a thirty-minute commute across town.

And then, of course, there is the voice inside your own head saying, *Everyone's partly right, but I'm the one who has to choose. It's my responsibility and if I don't choose right, I'm going to be letting everyone down. I'm going to be letting myself down.* And then the fear starts, and the second-guessing, and the guilt about the second-guessing.

Some might say that modern life asks men to make similar choices. But that doesn't stand up to much scrutiny. For all the dilemmas men face—and they have their share—there isn't much of a debate about whether they should put their work or family first. If they take an hour out of the day to meet their child at school, they're applauded. If they take a whole day, they're held up as exemplary models. And if they choose to stay at home, they have magazine articles written about them. They are free from the endless questioning, the finger-pointing, the blame, and the guilt that seem to accompany so many of the choices women make.

No, the pain and pressure of excess choice affects women more than men. And since no one wants to go back to a world with fewer choices, you have to learn the skill of making choices without fear, guilt, and regret. You have to learn how to use your choice-making to strengthen you.

Just Men

Yes, men are a chronic condition too. They aren't going away, and so you're going to have to learn how to live with them.

What exactly do men do to make your life more anxious and stress-filled? Well, some men don't cause those things. Some are just a joy to be around, a constant source of strength and satisfaction, emotionally supportive, perfectly in sync with you and your changing needs (all right, that may be pushing it a bit)—and those who do stress you out, whether husband, boss, friend, or colleague, will have their own peculiar ways of doing it.

However, having said this, there are some things that, in general, mankind does to womankind that can make your life harder than it necessarily needs to be.

Midlife Crisis

There's the fabled male midlife crisis, most often seen in middle-aged men's yearning for faster cars, more exhilarating hobbies, and younger wives. In my straw poll of women to whom I showed the U.S. General Social Survey graph—the one revealing that, as we age, women get sadder as men get happier—by far the most common explanation was that, in our society, a forty-eight-year-old man is in a much more powerful position than a forty-eight-year-old woman. Forty-eight-year-old men are supposedly just coming into the prime of their lives, financially and socially, whereas forty-eight-year-old women are supposedly becoming less relevant.

This crisis is actually quite difficult to pinpoint in the data. For example, ages at first and second marriage are virtually the same for men and women—men's first marriage occurs, on average, at age twenty-seven; women's at age twenty-five. Men are thirty-four when they get married a second time; women are thirty-two.[5] Anecdotally, though, one hears it all the time. Your experience may resonate with this anecdote or it may reject it—I hope the latter. But what's more important is that you face up to the fact that you cannot control what men do or don't do to act out their vulnerabilities. All you can do is take control of your own life and know yourself well enough to draw strength from the circumstances life presents you.

Housework

Housework, or the "second shift," as some women call it, is another source of stress. More specifically, that women do it and men don't.

According to the statistics, this isn't strictly true. It's not that men don't help with housework. It's just that they don't do quite as much of it as you do. In a typical week, 52 percent of women do some kind of housework; only 20 percent of men do. When it comes to cooking, 64 percent of women are doing something useful in the kitchen, compared to only 37 percent of men. And in terms of caring for the kids, women spend, on average, 1.2 hours a day playing with, dressing, bathing, changing, or doing homework with the kids, whereas men can muster only a third of that, 0.4 hours.[6]

No matter how you slice it, this is an unfair division of labor. It isn't healthy for women to be shouldering this much of the burden, and it doesn't have to be this way since there's nothing in men's DNA that says they can't do their fair share around the house. Fortunately, it doesn't look like it is staying this way—over the last forty years men have tripled the number of hours they devote to child care[7] and doubled how much housework they do.[8] This still leaves men doing a lot less than you, but as a qualified statistician, I have to tell you that the trend line is good. (Between 1975 and today, women's housework hours declined from twenty-one per week to seventeen, while men's jumped from six to thirteen.[9])

How can you speed up this trend? Some of it depends on how well you and your spouse communicate about who should do what, and how often, and how well—this conversation will have to focus on each of your strengths, and we'll deal with it directly in chapter 11. But the other thing you can do is keep working. The research is quite clear on this point: the longer a woman has worked outside the house—meaning the number of years you've worked, not the number of hours a week you work—the more housework and cooking and child care the man does.[10] Take your career seriously, and over time, it seems, so will he.

The Workplace

What about men in the workplace? Well, here we have a bad-news, good-news, bad-news situation. The bad news is that the world of work remains a world built mostly by men mostly for men. It is above all, a linear world. You put in the hours, you climb the ladder, you put in more hours, you climb still higher. But this linear path doesn't work as well for women. Whether you want children or not—and with more than 82 million mothers in America,[11] most women do—there's no escaping the fact that the clock expires on fertility. It's yet another decision you must make, a choice that impacts what career you follow and which positions you are willing to take.

I recently met up with a very smart friend of mine who trained to be a lawyer. Because Sarah was among the best of the best, she was hired by one of the most prestigious law firms in New York, a large firm employing over two thousand lawyers. Sarah was hired in a famous year for this law firm because it was the first time in the company's history that more than 50 percent of its 186 summer associates were women. Seven years later, not only had Sarah left, but so had all but two of the women they hired. Not one of her female contemporaries had stayed the course and been made partner. According to Sarah, this wasn't because the firm was actively discriminating against women; it was more that each individual woman had decided, somewhere along the way, that she was unwilling to devote herself to the job as exclusively as was required to make partner.

Clearly this is an extreme example, but it's telling. Women may place a premium on their working identities, but that's different from putting work at the center of their lives. When advancement depends on being able to work overtime, on a willingness always to be available, or on a decision to focus on work to the exclusion of everything else, plenty of women choose an option that enables them to pursue other goals and other roles that have meaning. They jump off the man-made ladder.

The good news is that this isn't stopping women from on-ramping back into work after having kids, in spite of media stories of a new generation of women choosing to opt out. Today, when women leave to have children, they return fast and in great numbers. In fact, in just one generation there's been an immense swing. In 1960, 14 percent of mothers were working six months after having a child. Now, 55 percent return in less than six months and 83 percent after one year.[12]

And, still in the good news column, these days many companies are spending considerable time and energy trying to incorporate the rhythms and schedules women want in a workplace. Onsite day care, telecommuting, flexible work options (FWOs), paid leave, and even a new organizational structure called the organizational lattice (as opposed to the organizational ladder) have become more prevalent in the last twenty years, and these options are likely to become even more popular as companies fight to recruit and retain the most talented women.

Firmly in the bad news column, however, is the discovery that most of these programs won't make you any happier. In fact, some studies examining the link between a woman's daily happiness and the availability of paid leave, telecommuting, and flexible work options reveal findings that are quite bleak: all of them—flex time, paid leave, telecommuting—have a *negative* correlation to your daily happiness.[13] To be clear, this means that if you telecommute or take advantage of a flexible schedule so that you can, say, drive the kids to school or pick them up, you are likely to be *less* happy than a woman working right next door to you in the same organization who doesn't.

Why is this so? A number of possible reasons. Maybe women who telecommute have a difficult time separating work life from home life and, with no natural breaks, they wind up blurring both and deriving satisfaction from neither. Maybe women who take advantage of paid leave are doing so because of other inherently stressful events in their life, such as having a baby or taking care of a sick relative. Maybe women who take advantage of flexible work options do so knowing that they are slipping onto the less prestigious mommy track, that in the corridors of power, FWO really stands for For Women Only.

Whatever the explanations, these findings *do not* imply that paid leave or telecommuting or flexible scheduling are actively detrimental to your happiness. They aren't. Used properly, in the right circumstances, and within a company culture that supports rather than marginalizes those who take advantage of them, these various programs can most certainly help you.

However, what they *do* imply is that you must not look to these programs as your cure-all. Neither the fact that your company offers these programs nor the fact that you actually use them has any measurable effect on how fulfilled you are in life. These programs, by themselves, won't make you happy. They won't guarantee you a strong life.

You're going to have to do that on your own.

It's Not the Hours

So to sum all this up, over the last forty years, many more choices and many more responsibilities have been added to your plate, but very few of the old ones have fallen away. You are now supposed to be a beautiful, adoring wife; a fantastic mother; a smart, aggressive career woman; and a hypercompetent administrator—or, if not all of the above all of the time, then at least you're supposed to be able to choose among these roles and balance the ones you've chosen.

And if you were to succeed in doing all this well, what would success look like? It'd look like a hybrid of Martha Stewart and Michelle Obama and Katie Couric and Meg Whitman and Angelina Jolie and Danica Patrick, all rolled into one unattainable package.

Yes, there has been some small lightening of your load—you may do less housework than you did, and your husband may help out a little more with the kids—but the ultimate responsibility for managing the house and the children's schedules still lands on your shoulders. It must feel as though you are working all the hours God gives.

And yet, counterintuitively, women today are not actually working more hours than they used to. Nor are they working more hours than men. Well, fair dues, you may in *your* household. But in a mammoth study of twenty-five countries, ranging from the U.S. to France to Slovenia to Madagascar, men and women were asked to keep track of what they were doing at various times during the day, and then the hours for each activity were calculated. The results: in developed countries, men average 5.2 hours of paid work a day, and 2.7 hours of home work, for a total of 7.9 hours a day; and women average 3.4 hours of paid work, and 4.5 hours of home work, for a total of, yes, 7.9 hours a day. These averages are statistically identical in virtually every developed country in the study: women and men work the same number of total hours in a day.[14]

It is only in less developed countries such as South Africa or Benin, where women have fewer choices and are largely excluded from the workplace, that women actually work more hours per day than men.

What this study suggests is that, though women have certainly become more stressed and anxious as they've taken on more roles and responsibilities during the last forty years, this creeping unhappiness is not caused by working longer hours.

Instead, think about it this way: The challenge of all the different roles you play is not that you don't have enough hours in the day. The challenge of all these roles is that during the hours you choose to work you have too many different things going on at any one time to focus properly on each of them. Your time isn't stretched; your attention is.

The Myth of Multitasking

To which, you may say, "I'm a great multitasker. I can pay attention to a bunch of things at the same time without skipping a beat." You may even say that this is a strength reserved for women, an evolutionary development that helped you fend off those saber-toothed tigers as you were feeding your kids. "I can bake a cake, finish the year-end report, and do seven loads of laundry while talking my best friend off the ledge."

You may think you can do this, and frankly, you may be right—a few of us have a uniquely powerful capacity for "disparate attention," to give multitasking its proper name. But the research on multitasking reveals that if you do truly excel at doing two things at once without any drop in quality or any increase in stress, you are in a minority.

The human brain is simply not designed to multitask. You can get by doing multiple things at once, but you can't do them well. Your brain is physically unable to process more than one set of instructions at a time, so while you are juggling all of those actions at once, your brain is scrambling to keep up. Through a variety of experiments measuring brain activity, scientists have discovered that the constant switching back and forth from one activity to another energizes regions of the brain that specialize in visual processing and physical coordination, while simultaneously disrupting the brain regions related to memory and learning. According to the research, "we are using our mental energy to concentrate on concentrating at the expense of whatever it is that we're supposed to be concentrating on."[15] Got that?

More simply: when we multitask we're dumber. How much dumber? A recent study for Hewlett Packard exploring the impact of multitasking on performance revealed that the average worker's functioning IQ drops ten points when multitasking, more than double the four-point drop that occurs when someone smokes marijuana. (The analogy the researchers used is that a ten-point drop in IQ is equivalent to missing one night of sleep.)[16]

It's an obvious irony. You're trying to get more done in less time but, in reality, multitasking actually slows you down.

It also increases your stress. Many studies have found that multitasking boosts the level of stress-related hormones such as cortisol and adrenaline, and it wears down your system, prematurely aging you. Cortisol has also been linked to increased belly fat. So, in the short term, the confusion and fatigue merely hamper your ability to think clearly, but in the long term, the effects can be much more damaging.

If your ready-made solution to the variety of roles you play is multitasking, you are shortchanging everyone in your life. You most of all.

We know that women's overall life satisfaction trends downward over the course of her life. We know that multitasking is not the best way to reverse this trend. Nor is organizing time better. Nor is working harder. Nor is participating in company-sponsored programs. Nor is turning back the clock to a time of fewer choices and opportunities.

We know the solution must have something to do with how you choose to pay attention. It must be something over which you have control. It must be something that helps you in all the roles you are required to play. And it must be something that strengthens you, rather than depletes you, as you get older.

Let's dive into it.

WHAT TO TAKE AWAY FROM THIS CHAPTER

- **Over the last forty years women have gained more opportunities and more responsibilities.** Very few, if any, have been relinquished. Consequently, your greatest challenge in life is to make wise choices.

- **More choice doesn't correlate to more happiness.** More choice can, in fact, add to your levels of stress and make your life harder.

- **The policies and programs created to accommodate many women's need for more flexible scheduling have shown either no correlation or a negative correlation to a woman's daily levels of happiness.**

- **In developed countries, women and men work the same number of hours.** Women's increasing levels of stress seem to be caused less by the actual number of hours worked, than by the sheer variety of what has to happen within those hours. Stress is caused by trying to pay attention to too many different responsibilities at once.

- **The ability to multi-task with no loss of quality and no increase in stress is extremely rare.** And, where it does exist, it is no more likely to be found in women than in men. (It is also dangerous. Research by the National Highway Traffic Safety Administration reveals that if you are talking on the phone while driving—even hands-free—you are four times more likely do be in an accident than if you are not. In fact, the accident rate of phone-talking drivers is the same as drivers whose alcohol level is .08—legally drunk.)

PART 2

LEARN TO LIVE YOUR STRONGEST LIFE

SIGNS OF LIFE

What does a strong life actually feel like?

Life begets life. Energy creates energy. It is by
spending oneself that one becomes rich.

—SARAH BERNHARDT (1844–1923), French actress

've interviewed thousands of effective women over the last twenty years, and the frustrating thing (from a researcher's perspective) is they look so very different. Some are employed full-time and have their kids in day care. Some stay at home. Some used to stay at home while their kids were young but now have on-ramped back into the workforce. Some have broken through the increasingly cracked glass ceiling at work and are now running the whole organization, while others are content to see their work as peripheral. Some are happy clambering up the corporate ladder, while others have long ago jumped off the ladder and found fulfillment in running their own business or devoting themselves to charity work.

Anna Carson is living a strong life. She's wife to her husband, David, mother to Ben and Charlotte, the administrator of Ben's baseball team, and, at the same time, a top agent in Hollywood, a power player in one of the most cutthroat of businesses.

Wendy Stafford is living a strong life. With three kids at home and a working husband, she is the principal of a school in Memphis, Tennessee. Reading the hundreds of posts from unhappy teachers on the Oprah.com message boards, you would be forgiven for thinking that teaching and life satisfaction were mutually exclusive, but not for Wendy. She's a dynamic force for change at her school, bubbling over with enthusiasm at the challenge of leading a team of two hundred teachers, caring for a diverse student body, and ensuring that her school meets all the metrics mandated by No Child Left Behind.

Gina Light is living a strong life. She's a senior vice president of marketing for one of the largest toy makers in the world. She has three kids under fifteen, a husband who works seventy hours a week in the restaurant business, and she commutes twice a month from the West Coast to her company's offices in Rhode Island. Her schedule would burn out most of us, but when you talk to her, her eyes are alive and excited. Clearly she loves her bicoastal work-family life.

Candace Nelson is living a strong life. After quitting her job during the dot-com bust a few years ago, she and her husband, Charles, decided to set up a bakery making only cupcakes. It was a risky venture—cupcakes? In these health-conscious times? It'll never work! But today her one store has grown into five; people line the street to taste her specialty, red velvet; and she is happy that her most recent addition, her twenty-one-month-old son, Charlie, gets to see his mommy doing what she loves.

Maggie Mosely is living a strong life. I met her on the Oprah show. She worked in the packaging field and was unhappy that this male-dominated industry was preventing her from getting the promotion she thought she deserved. After the show, she realized it wasn't the industry as a whole; it was just her company. So, after seventeen years with this company, she quit, polished her résumé, and sought out an organization that would value her for her performance. Immediately she got four job offers, took one, and when I spoke with her recently, she had just received a large bonus for closing a deal for L'Oréal's packaging business.

I could go on, and I'm sure you could add a few examples from your own circle of friends. And if you did, and if you looked closely, you'd immediately see that a strong life isn't necessarily a wealthy life, a career-focused life, a stay-at-home life, or a married life. It can't be defined by a particular job, field, income bracket, or number of hours worked. It can't be defined by any of those things because a strong life isn't what you do. It's what you feel.

And when you examine what each of these women feel, suddenly they all sound the same. It's not that they are all beatifically happy—as I mentioned earlier there is some research to suggest that those who rate themselves an eight or nine out ten on a happiness scale are actually more effective and fulfilled than those who rate themselves a full ten out of ten. A strong life is not a life of utter contentment

However, look closely and you find they share four emotions in common.

Successful

A strong woman feels successful. And by "successful," I don't mean that she is getting prizes, awards, and big fat bonuses—though she might be. I mean that she feels effective and capable. She feels that many of the activities filling her weeks are things she's good at, activities that give her a chance to express her strengths. This is tremendously important because each of us is blessed with unique strengths, and these strengths demand to be expressed. A strong life must give you regular outlets for and affirmations of these strengths—without these, you will start to lose your sense of who you really are and what you are capable of.

Sustaining this feeling of being successful is difficult for a woman if she quits the world of work to become a full-time mom. Although this new role may square with her values, it's hard to feel successful as a mom for three reasons:

1. Mothers often hide their imperfections from one another ("Oh really? No, it's not a problem for us. We get the kids to bed every night at 6:30 sharp") and tend to mercilessly exaggerate the perfections of their little ones ("Oh yes, he's been sleeping through the night since he was six weeks old").

2. There are so many different vantage points from which to judge your success as a mom. Your kids, your mother, and your friends think you're great, but your husband doesn't; your husband, kids, and mother think you're supermom, but your friends don't; your friends, your mother, and your husband are happy, but you don't "get" your kids; ad infinitum, through a million different permutations. With all these conflicting viewpoints, no wonder mothers struggle to get a firm fix on whether they are truly successful.

3. While your role at work may well have given you the

chance to express your unique combination of strengths, your role as mother may not.

Instinctive Anticipation

A strong woman instinctively looks forward to tomorrow. I don't mean she jumps out of bed every morning raring to go—a physical impossibility when you've stayed up till one in the morning organizing your daughter's soccer photos and she wakes you up at 4:00 a.m. complaining of a stomachache, and then the same thing happens the very next night. I simply mean she positively anticipates the next day. She feels hope, excitement, even joy, when she thinks about the near-term future. It's a gut-level sense of being on the right track and of enjoying the ride, bumps and all.

Growing and Learning

A strong woman feels she is still learning and growing, no matter her age. She may be taking classes at work or at home, or she may simply be learning on the job, but no matter where the growth is coming from, she reports that she is getting better at something. And accompanying this feeling of growth is a sense of focus, an ability to concentrate. Time, she says, seems to speed up, and many times during the course of a week she will look up after what seems like five minutes and discover that a whole hour has passed by.

Psychologists label this feeling "flow." It is one of the most important signs that you are living a strong life.

In contrast, when the present moment stretches on forever,

when each moment seems irrevocably detached from the next, when your prevailing feeling is one of stagnation or distraction, when you and your life feel dull, psychologists have another term for it: "depression."

Needs Fulfilled

A strong woman feels that her needs are fulfilled. She may sometimes feel tired—and given all the roles women are expected to play today, who wouldn't?—but she doesn't feel overwhelmed and empty. In fact she feels the opposite of empty. She feels filled up. Her purpose needs are met—she feels she is doing what she is supposed to be doing, however imperfectly. Her relationship needs are met—she has a loving husband, a supportive boss, a caring group of friends. And her recognition needs are met—someone within her circle of intimates is celebrating her successes and reinforcing her strengths.

SIGNs of a Strong Life

These are the emotional signs you are living a strong life:

- Successful
- Instinctively looking forward to tomorrow
- Growing and learning
- Needs fulfilled

Everything we're going to talk about in this book will be targeted toward helping you feel these four feelings. Think of the acronym SIGN to fix these feelings in your mind.

WHAT TO TAKE AWAY FROM THIS CHAPTER

- A strong woman is not necessarily happy one hundred percent of the time.
- A strong life isn't what you do, it's what you feel.
- Strong women do not make the same life choices, but they do end up sharing the same four feelings.
- They feel successful, an instinctive anticipation, a sense that they are learning and growing, and that their most important needs are being met.
- **To measure how strongly a person feels these emotions, we have relied on five questions.** We have asked these questions of tens of thousands of women (and men) in the US, the UK, Canada, China, Japan, and India. We will extend our research to more countries in the near future.
  - How often do you feel an emotional high in your life?
  - How often do you find yourself positively anticipating your day?
  - How often do you become so involved in what you are doing that you lose track of time?
  - How often do you feel invigorated at the end of a long, busy day?
  - How often do get to do things you really like to do?
- **To assess how strong your life is at the moment, you can ask yourself these questions.** The happiest and most successful women find that they can honestly say "everyday" to at least four out of the five.

5

A STRONG LIFE LIVED

What does a strong life actually look like?

We all live in suspense, from day to day, from hour to
hour; in other words, we are the hero of our own story.

—MARY MCCARTHY (1912–1989), American writer

No matter how strong you are feeling right now—you might be
in your strengths zone or completely lost—your challenge is
straightforward: how can you design your life so that, week by
week, it strengthens you? Faced with a world that expects so much of
you, but that is blind to who you are and what you really need, how
can you be true to yourself? How can you live the life you were supposed to live?

Look around you—you probably have already—and you will find
some wonderfully helpful advice, everything from time management
to defining personal boundaries, all the way to spiritual advice about
building a life of faith.

Though a lot of this advice is excellent, I have been looking for
something different. What, if anything, do women who are both
happy and successful have in common? Not that they will have all

made the same choices in life—they clearly haven't—but they might have all had a similar method to making their choices, whatever they turned out to be.

Do they all have the same *approach*?

I believe they do. This approach explains not only why they make the choices they do, but also why these choices carry strength and power, rather than guilt and regret. This approach is a *practice*, not a destination; and as with any practice, if you stop doing it, you won't net the outcomes you want. But when you stick with it, and learn to get good at it, this strong-life practice will help you make the right choices in virtually every aspect and stage of your life. I realize that's quite a lot to ask of one practice, but read on and you'll see that this strong-life practice can indeed become your master lever: pull it, and everything in your life will work better.

It can benefit both men and women, but since, at its core, it is a practice that shows you how to *choose*, and since women have many more choices to make than men, it will benefit women most.

In this next section, you will see what this practice looks like and, hopefully, learn how to incorporate it into your own life.

To introduce it to you, I'll ask you to put on your researcher's hat for a few minutes. Rather than simply asking you to take the Strong Life test and describing in bald terms what this strong-life practice entails, let me tell you the story of two women. If you really want to understand what it takes to live a happy and fulfilling life, it's worth getting to know them. You see, they are similar in many ways. Both were born and raised in the Midwest; both earned college degrees; both are healthy and have a wide circle of friends; both are smart, articulate, and funny. Both are married, and both have two kids, a boy and a girl. But at the time we meet them, they feel completely different about their lives.

You may recall Anna Carson in the last chapter. She's the Hollywood agent. When you think of her, don't imagine a slick, Gucci-clad, deal-making shark. Instead picture a tall redhead, quick to smile, with a hearty laugh. A woman who doesn't necessarily demand your attention when she walks into a room, but who reveals her strength and self-assurance in each subsequent meeting. She's really competent, and she knows it. Yet not in an arrogant way. Her manner is so open, so candid, so optimistic, she leaves you feeling that she would be a great best friend. You know you would trust her with your career, and more. And as you chat with her, listening to her self-deprecating stories of motherhood and movie-land, you can't help it, the cliché question pops into your head—*How does she do it?*

Meeting Charlie prompts a very different question: *What can I possibly do to help her?* She's about five years older than Anna and somehow she's slid into a life that doesn't fit her at all, a life where she feels a toxic combination of panicked, incompetent, and, in the end, numb.

She explains, "I'm working as the office manager for my husband's company. He felt I was the only one he could really trust, and besides it would give me the chance to be there with the kids after they came home from school, so I took the job. But it's killing me. I feel most unhappy knowing that I am disappointing the people who mean the most to me. When I take a personal inventory, I realize I traded my professional life for a better personal life and now my personal life is suffering too. I'm completely stuck. I know I need to leave this job, but I don't know how to quit my company without quitting my marriage."

You could theorize until you're blue in the face about what it takes to live a strong life, but one way to think about it is to ask yourself, "What's the difference between Anna's actions and Charlie's?" Both started off in roughly the same situation, yet one ended up motivated and fulfilled, while the other (at the time I met her) recoils at the thought of waking up tomorrow and going to work. What can account for this difference?

In looking at both women, you might say that the wild card in their game of life was good fortune—Anna had it; Charlie didn't—and you might be right. Luck certainly played some role in how their lives turned out, as it did, does, and will in yours.

Or you might say that one chose the "right" career, and the other didn't. Or that one chose to stay in the Midwest while the other moved to L.A. Or you might land on some other explanation, some other variable. And in each case, you might be right.

What I must tell you, though, is that I interviewed a lot of women who were happy and successful, and a lot who, at the time, were less so, and that, Anna and Charlie best capture the difference between the two groups. Look closely at the choices each made and how they made them, and you'll see that Anna took a distinct approach to her life, different from Charlie's, and this approach—more than any other variable—explains why she made the choices she did, and why these choices strengthened her.

Charlie's not to blame for her choices—she is a driven, well-intentioned woman doing her best in a world that doesn't know her. Nor am I saying that Anna followed this approach all the time—as you'll see, there were long stretches of her life where she neglected it. What I am saying is that whenever—and there were multiple times—Anna needed to get her life on track, it was this approach, this practice, that did it for her, and that when Charlie's life went wrong, it was a flawed approach that led her astray.

Charlie

Charlie had always had a passion for developing teenagers, in particular kids who were struggling. So after graduating with a degree in English, she worked to get the qualifications necessary to become a therapeutic recreation specialist, someone who used outdoor activities and games to rehabilitate juvenile sex offenders.

With her qualifications in hand, she made the leap to the world of recreational rehab. And for a while she found it quite rewarding. Yes, the kids could be mentally exhausting, but she was energized by the thought that she was bringing comfort and aid to those whom society had cast aside.

Two questions nagged at her, though. First, she wasn't making very much money. She had a nice house, but it was in a questionable part of town, the kind of neighborhood where everything looks fine on the surface but you can't let your kids play in the front yard. She was a single mom by this point, so, financially, she was feeling a little anxious.

Also, aspects of the recreational therapy job were starting to get to her. One of the boys she was working closely with had recently committed suicide and another had tried to stab her with a pen. There were days when the job was just a little too intense.

She was sizing up her options when she met Peter. He ran a small engineering consulting organization in their town, and the moment they met, they knew their relationship had the potential for something special. They were both outdoorsy and loved sailing and camping. On any Friday night Peter would turn to Charlie and say, "Let's go," and in forty-five minutes, without a word needed between them, they would pack up everything and be ready to head out for a weekend trip. Both of them knew how rare it was to find a partner with whom they were so completely in sync.

Peter loved how clear and systematic a thinker Charlie was. "Come work with me," he said. "Come help me organize our work flow. Get our systems up and running. I've got no one to turn to, no one I can rely on."

"Besides," he went on, half joking, "it'll be a great litmus test for our relationship."

No pressure there, Charlie thought. But, then again, she did love Peter, and she was intrigued by designing programs and systems—when she wasn't camping or sailing she could be found trawling the Barnes and Noble stacks looking for the latest tome on systems integration. (It sounds odd, I know, but trust me: for Charlie there's nothing quite like reading a good systems integration book to pass the time.) Sure, it was an office environment and she'd never worked in one of those, but it would offer her more flexibility, the chance to spend more time with her kids, to pick them up from school, and to be there when they played in the front yard. *Maybe things will work out with Peter*, she thought, *and we'll move in with him, out of this part of town, and everything will be great.*

Initially, things did work out according to Charlie's plan. She and Peter were married a year later, they did move to a safer part of town, and at work she proved her value by redesigning the entire office work flow. With her ability to gain a thirty-thousand-foot perspective on the company's operations, she was able to design a system where everyone—employees, clients, Peter himself—could track the status of any project and the clients were automatically matched up with the right employees whenever they called with questions or concerns.

But then Peter asked her to come in and run the systems she had built. Be the office manager. Do the accounting. Pay the taxes. Handle the invoicing and the collections. Be his right hand.

And gradually things started to fall apart.

This was her description of her life when I first met her: "I take no pleasure in a reconciled bank account; in fact, I dread the financial responsibilities that have become mine and mine alone. I hate the repetition of the day-to-day tasks. I don't like being interrupted by one area of my job when my head is deep into another area. I tend to have a loud voice (camp counselor, recreation leader voice), and I don't have good phone etiquette, and when you add to that the fact that my office is open to everyone else and I am constantly on the phone dealing with sensitive financial or personnel issues, you have a terrible work environment. I feel crushed whenever I receive a comment about the appearance of my desk, speaking too loud and not being discreet with financial information, or getting nothing more done than the day-to-day, never doing anything to grow the business."

She made countless plans to talk with Peter about her growing unhappiness, but she couldn't find the right words or the right way to frame the conversation. She knew he didn't feel comfortable letting anyone else see the financials of the business, and she took his trust very seriously. And of course, she was *capable* of balancing a checkbook and paying the invoices. But how would she even broach the subject? "Honey, I love you and I know you need me to do this, and I know, do I ever, how overwhelmed you are, but I just don't like paying these invoices. I just don't like keeping my desk organized. I just don't like opening all these envelopes."

It sounded ridiculous, pathetic even. And "pathetic" she wasn't. Charlie had always seen herself as a positive, confident, self-reliant person. She had always taken care of her family. She didn't need help or a handout from anybody. She was strong, she could cope, she was fine, thank you very much. She wasn't about to whine to her husband about how her job was "getting her down," particularly not with him working so hard right by her side. "If I change my attitude," she said to herself, "look on the bright side, organize myself a little better, I can make it through this trying time and get to the other side."

And yet today, at this moment right now, she knows, with as much certainty as she knows anything, "I should not be doing this job."

She admits that she tried to dismiss this certainty, banish it to a small, dark corner of her mind, and cover it up with happy, grateful thoughts. But it refused to stay hidden. It kept pushing itself to the forefront of her mind, insisting, "I should not be doing this job. I must get out of this situation. I must talk to Peter."

But she didn't. The conversation kept getting delayed. There was never a good time or a good way that she could see to talk about it. And then a horrible event occurred—her daughter's best friend committed suicide—and Charlie was consumed with making sure her daughter and her schoolmates were grieving in a way that was healthy, not self-punishing. Her daughter's friend had called the night before the suicide, but her daughter hadn't called back. When she did return the call the next morning, her friend was already dead. Charlie found herself spending many hours a week at school sitting with her daughter and her friends, counseling them, helping them to grapple with the anger and the confusion.

This felt authentic to Charlie—after all, she was a therapist for troubled teenagers. What else was she supposed to do now that her daughter and her schoolmates were suffering? But it meant that *her* life, and the conversation with Peter, got pushed even further down the list of must-dos. Down and down it went. Months passed during which her panicky little fears swelled into full overwhelm, then dulled into numbness, and she slowly emptied herself out, until one day, Charlie broke. Stopped. Crumpled. Couldn't put her key in the car door and drive to work.

She checked herself into the hospital and that, for a while, was that.

Charlie is an extreme example, but you've probably seen friends get themselves into similar situations. They don't do anything wrong— at least not on the surface. More often than not, they are trying to do the *right* thing—support their husband, earn more money, be there for the kids. All of these are noble intentions, and they are certainly what drove Charlie. And, before things started to go wrong, it would have been a bold confidant who would have told her to ignore these noble intentions and do something else.

Yet we now know that Charlie followed through on all these intentions and still wound up living the opposite of a strong life—no success, no instinctive anticipation, no growth, and very few needs fulfilled.

There must have been a better way, something she could have done before she started down the wrong path. And if not, surely she could have done something to stop the sinking and resuscitate her life.

What would you have told her to do? Just gut it up and have the conversation? Easy to say, but very hard to do when that conversation is fraught with other, conflicting emotions, such as "I've got to be there for my husband" and "I've got to do the right thing for my kids." What she needed was a way to fulfill her obligations as a wife and mother and, at the same time, honor her own strengths and passions. She needed a new approach to seeing her life and making her choices. She needed a new practice.

Anna

Anna's life and the choices she made offer clues to what would have helped Charlie. As you read her story, don't imagine that Anna has led a picture-perfect life, a life that you or Charlie or anyone else should copy. As I said before, it's been a regular sort of life, with confused beginnings, long stretches of "What am I doing with my life?" and the occasional "Oh no, what have I done!" The lesson from Anna's life is not that she never felt confused or lost or weak; instead, the lesson lies in how she made her choices whenever these feelings came upon her. Her intentions were as noble as Charlie's were, but her approach was different, and so her choices were different, and so her life was different.

Anna Carson grew up not in the shadow of the Hollywood sign but on a farm in Iowa. Her dad was a farmer, and her childhood address was the kind of thing you make up when you're making up stories about farmers: The Carson Farm, Rural Route 1, Iowa City, Iowa.

Anna was the fourth child out of six, the girl in the middle, and her family was close and tight-knit. So when she was ready to go to college, she chose the University of Iowa. It was home.

And she did well; she's always been a hard worker. She graduated with a degree in business administration, which she used to get a job as a district supervisor for a high-end grocery chain. That seemed the right thing to do at the time. It gave her a car, a steady income, a place to live close to her family, and a future that was already mapping itself out.

But then something happened, an event that became a critical catalyst in Anna's story. One day, she saw a shoplifter on the store's closed-circuit television. Anna called the police, but because she was one of six and not afraid to stand up for herself, she decided to confront the man alone. She challenged him, and he seemed about to 'fess up and give in, when suddenly he turned and sprinted down the aisle toward the front of the store. Unthinking, Anna dashed after him, caught him—did I mention she's tall and long-legged?—and grabbed his shoulder, at which point he twisted in her grip, punched her full in the mouth, and escaped.

She stumbled back to her office, called the police again, and tried to speak. Blood-spittle and gargled words were all she could manage, so she hung up and pulled out a mirror from her desk drawer to assess the damage. She wasn't in much pain (mouth injuries are funny that way; you don't feel much pain until the oral surgeon starts giving you Novocain injections), but she could see that all four of her front teeth had been smashed up. And there in her office, as she sat waiting for the police to arrive, feeling out the damage with her tongue, she found herself thinking, *What on earth am I doing here in this job, in this store, in Iowa? Is this seriously what I want for my life? To be a grocery-chain supervisor five miles from where I grew up?*

Anna loved her family. Her mother, despite losing both of her own parents when she was only nine years old, was optimistic and enthusiastic, an endlessly positive influence on Anna's life. Her dad was the farmer, cautious, aware that the wind and weather will change. In his world, you plant your seeds and you wait for them to grow. It's what he thought Anna should do: settle with the seeds she had sown, build her reputation, and secure her future.

So what did she do? Sorry, Mom and Dad, Anna listened to her instincts and followed her boyfriend to Washington, D.C., where he was getting his master's degree at George Washington University.

When she arrived, she hunted around for work. She still wasn't sure what she wanted to do with her life, but that didn't stop her from getting a job. That's one thing Anna always believed in. You always find something to do to move forward, even if you know it isn't what you are going to be doing for the rest of your life.

So she found the best temp job she could, working for the Paper and Plastics Association, as it happens, and all was fine and dandy. Washington, D.C. was a fun place for a couple of young, upwardly mobile Iowans—when, out of the blue, her boyfriend landed a job as an associate professor in a small university town in Germany.

Should she go? *Well,* she thought, *why not? I haven't yet found my purpose in life, and since I moved to D.C. for him, why wouldn't I go in whole hog and move to Germany with him?* So she did, and as before, when she arrived, she rustled up some work. This was trickier to pull off than it had been in D.C. because, technically, she wasn't allowed to work, but she ferreted around anyway and soon she was teaching English and aerobics, helping a German friend file for a United States visa, and basically gaining a pretty good foothold, when, after a short nine months, her boyfriend announced that Germany wasn't working out for him, that they should move back to the U.S. He was thinking Denver, Colorado—what did she think?

She thought they should give Germany a fair shot. But, still playing the dutiful girlfriend role, she swallowed that opinion and hightailed it to Denver. Where, upon arrival, her boyfriend decided that eight years was enough. The relationship was over.

Now what was she going to do? She was twenty-nine, single, and aimless. Talk to your friends or visit the Oprah.com message boards, and you'll hear stories from thousands of women in similar predicaments. They moved their lives around for a boyfriend or a husband, and then, after the break-up, they found themselves at a loss. This other person had given their lives direction and purpose, so they didn't have to ask themselves too many questions about what *their* strengths were, what *they* wanted to do with *their* lives, what *their* destiny was. But now, with that person gone, those questions crescendo until they can't think about anything else.

This is what happened to Anna. She sat herself down and forced herself to ask all those destiny, purpose, and "what should I do with my life?" questions.

And then a false start. Having racked her brains for something to latch on to and coming up empty, she took another temping job, this one on the TV show *COPS*. She was quickly promoted to onsite producer, yet almost immediately she knew she'd made a mistake. The job had superficial trappings of glamour—this was television, after all—but its core purpose grated on her. Some people get a jolt of energy from filming reality shows. They love the rawness and the unpredictability of it. But Anna didn't. She saw herself as a voyeur of Denver's underbelly, someone who was profiting from her subjects' suffering. When she filmed a person who was arrested for DUI, he or she was *really* arrested. When she captured a person being carted away to jail, he was *really* being carted away. Was this where her life was meant to end up? Was this why she had worked for her degree, why she had defied the advice of her parents and followed a man around the world? Her instinctive answer was no, so with no clear alternative in mind, she quit.

It was while she was weighing her future, and fending off anxious inquiries from her mom—

"Are you sure you want to quit, honey? It's a good job."

"Yes, Mom. I'm sure."

"You haven't really found your feet since you left Iowa. Maybe it's time to come back and rethink things."

"No, Mom. I'm fine, really."

—that Anna took a New Year's trip to visit her sister in Chicago. And there, at 2:00 a.m. on New Year's Day, she met the man who would become her husband, David. David was in sales for his family's printing business and was about to relocate to Los Angeles. By the time he was due to go, he and Anna were in a serious relationship, both sure they had found a life partner in the other. So, with a *here-we-go-again* feeling, Anna followed her man to a new city where she knew no one, had no leads, no contacts, and no idea of what to do.

Back to the destiny, purpose, and "what should I do with my life?" questions. Sitting around the apartment they'd rented, she dredged through her life trying to find something, anything that might give her a clue about how to bring focus to her willingness to work hard. All she could come up with was that she was an inveterate clipper. A confessed "information junkie," she would clip articles from any publication she happened to be reading (this was pre-Internet) and stack them in file folders for . . . well, who knows what they were for? She just liked having information at her fingertips.

She pulled out the file folders from one of the moving boxes (the clippings traveled with her from Iowa via D.C., Germany, and Denver) and sifted through them. And as she was doing that—as she pulled each one out, reread it, and carefully put it aside—she had a vivid memory of looking at a huge magazine stand at the University of Iowa, reaching past John Deere's *Tractor Quarterly* and *Cosmopolitan*, and picking the *Hollywood Reporter* from the racks. And not just one time. Often. Once a week at least. Thinking back now, she remembered that she wouldn't read the first two or three pages, the ones with the stories about the biggest stars of the day and their exploits. Instead, she would turn to the back of the magazine and read about the details of the deals. How did this movie get financed? Which studio bought this book to adapt into a movie? Who was going to direct it? How much would they get paid?

It seemed crazy that she'd forgotten this, but with all the flitting around the world and the scrabbling for work and the traipsing after her boyfriend, she had. Now, as she sat quietly reading the clippings—here was one about the setting up of the Disney Channel; here was one about the making of *Beverly Hills Cop*—it came back to her with great vividness. *Huh*, she thought. *Interesting. I really like learning about the details of movie business deals.*

She didn't know what job she should try to get, but at least she had something authentic to build upon. And while she had no connections and no film experience, at least she was in the right town to start discovering what she wanted to build.

She asked around in some employment agencies and was told, "If you want to learn the ropes, become an assistant to a talent agent. You'll probably hate it—they'll make you scurry around like a mad four-year-old—but there's no better or faster way to gain experience in the entertainment industry."

So Anna thought, *All right, I'll treat it as an MBA in the entertainment industry. I'll work as seriously as I can for three years and then take stock.* She had heard of a company that promoted from within its ranks, so she applied there for an assistant's job and was hired to work for a book agent.

"From almost the day I arrived, I knew I was at the right place," Anna says. "There was a book that my boss was trying to buy for a producer, and as her assistant I got to see the whole thing unfold. I was at the center of it all as we negotiated with the author of the book, hooked in a screenwriter, and closed the deal with the production company. I can still remember holding the author's $1 million check in my hand. But it wasn't the money that excited me; it was being at the center of things. Being the hub. I just loved that I knew more than everyone else about what was going on."

Fueled by this love, her new role consumed her. While other assistants were out at parties, schmoozing and networking, Anna stayed late at work, gathering information, planning, devising ways for the agency to do better, writing ideas and notes for her boss at midnight. Looking back, she realizes she was probably something of a nuisance, but she couldn't help herself. The ideas came so furiously she just had to capture them and share them with whoever would listen. *Finally*, she thought, *my real life has started.*

And then a setback. One of the ideas she presented to her boss was that the company needed a coordinator for her department, someone who would gather all the relevant information about each of the agency's clients and then use it to position the right client with the right project no matter where the client or the project resided within the agency. This position didn't exist at the agency, and, in Anna's opinion, this meant many opportunities to find good work for their clients were missed. She told a couple of people about her idea and was waiting for the right moment to tell her boss, when an announcement was made that another assistant, a friend she'd shared her idea with, had been given the role. Apparently this "friend" had made an appointment with the powers-that-be, presented the idea as his, and soon thereafter been offered the position.

Anna was floored. She'd trusted this person, confided in him, and then he'd stolen not only her idea but the position as well. How could she have been so naive? She was thirty years old. She should have known better.

She kicked herself. Stomped around the apartment. Shouted her frustrations at David. Fantasized about creative methods of retribution.

And then she righted herself. She could have raised a stink about it and demanded a fair hearing, but talking it through with David, she decided to take a different tack. She knew three things for sure: (1) the agency needed this coordinator role not just within her department but within other departments as well; (2) she was still the best person for this kind of "information junkie" role; and (3) if she just kept talking up the role and making others see how useful it could be, in the end, other opportunities would present themselves.

On all three counts, she was right. Six months after her "perfect" job was stolen from her, the agency created the same role for another department—the talent department (think movie stars)—and offered her the job.

"Everyone in the talent department was shocked," she remembers with a smile. "They were like 'Who's this assistant from the literary department, and why did she get this job?' They didn't realize that I'd been laying the groundwork for the last nine months or more."

Fast-forward a year and a half, and Anna was excelling in the coordinator role. In fact, she was getting so good and feeling so confident in her abilities that she allowed herself to start wondering when she'd be promoted to the plum role of talent agent.

This role is the lifeblood of the agency. Everything depends on the agent's ability both to sign quality clients and then to find good work for these clients. And Anna was certain that she would excel at it. In fact, in her estimation, she was already doing the work—she had studied the intricacies of every deal that came across her desk; she was known to have a wealth of information at her fingertips and so was regularly sought out by clients and agents alike; and, most importantly, people trusted her.

So she asked her boss when she was going to be promoted. "Soon," she was told.

Then she asked again.

And again. And again. Always politely. And always armed with an example or two about how she was already doing the job.

"Soon," she was told.

And so, finally, she gave the agency an ultimatum. It was done very professionally, but it was an ultimatum nonetheless: "I'm doing the agent job now; I just don't have the title. Give me the title by June, or I will go be an agent somewhere else."

Whether worn down by her persistence or persuaded by her obvious competence, or a combination of the two, when the June deadline hit—and not a week earlier—they made her a full agent.

That was a decade ago, and during those years Anna has risen to become one of the most trusted and influential agents in Hollywood.

One final detail: Not long after she became an agent, Anna became a mother too, giving birth to her son, Ben. She nursed him and after her maternity leave was up, she returned to the agency. Both she and David had full-time jobs, so, as many working couples do, they hired a nanny.

She explains, "I thought I'd be fine with it, and I guess I was for a while. But then my senses started picking up on something. I felt weird leaving him. It's not that I didn't want to go back to work—I did, and I enjoyed work even after being a mom. It's just that something didn't seem quite right at home. I wrestled with it for a couple of weeks trying to pin it down. And then one morning, it dawned on me that our nanny was rushing me out of the house. It wasn't anything that I could actually point to; it was just a feeling, a feeling that grew more insistent the more I thought about it: 'My nanny does not want me in my house!'"

She installed a nanny-cam. And that night, watching it at home— "The worst night of my life," she calls it—she saw why the nanny wanted her out of there. The nanny slept on the floor for almost the entire day.

"It killed me to see video of Ben clambering over her and toddling to the window calling our names, looking over the little gate into the kitchen and calling for me. It wasn't that she was being mean to him. She was just completely ignoring him. No attention. No love. No cuddling. Absolutely nothing. It was just terrible. The next morning, the full mama bear came out, and I fired her the moment she set foot in our house."

Which left her and David with a problem. Anna didn't want to stop working, but neither could she stomach the thought of leaving Ben at home. Even with a different nanny. She and David sat down that night and talked it out. It was a tough night, but in the end they found the right solution for them. As much as Anna loved her job, David was bored with his—his family had sold the printing business and the new owners weren't overly fond of having the oldest son still walking the halls. David, this athletic, rangy six-foot-three-inch sportsman, didn't know what it would be like to spend all day looking after his son, but he wanted to give it a try. Anna would work full-time, he would take care of Ben and any other kids who came along (a daughter, Charlotte, after a couple of years), and then Anna would come home and put them to bed every night.

That was seven years ago. It's not an arrangement that would work for every family, but it works for Anna and David. They are lucky to have each other, and they are stronger together.

What's the Difference?

What can you learn from comparing Anna's life with Charlie's? The differences aren't immediately obvious, are they?

Drive? No, both Anna and Charlie were driven. And besides, I imagine you know lots of driven individuals, some of whom are not happy, some of whom are not successful, and some of whom are neither.

How about a caring partner? You might think to yourself that Anna was uniquely blessed, with David giving up his job and looking after the kids. But her blessings aren't as unique as you might think—according to the most recent U.S. census, in 20 percent of households the primary caregiver for children in kindergarten or younger was the husband, and in 35 percent of households the wife earns more than the husband. Besides, if David had decided not to stay home, or if they couldn't have afforded for him to quit his job, I see Anna as the kind of person who would have figured out another workable solution, don't you?

And what about David in comparison to Charlie's partner, Peter? Having talked at length to all four of them, I have to tell you that Peter appears just as loving and caring as David. Even if he weren't, is a caring partner really the deciding factor in your success and happiness? A caring relationship is a beautiful gift, but many times a caring partner and a strong life do not go hand in hand—in fact, sometimes a caring partner encourages our very worst decisions.

Following your passion? Passion is surely somewhere to be found at the heart of a strong life, but, then again, your passions often compete with one another. Charlie was passionate about Peter and her family, yet she was not passionate about her work. Which passion should she sacrifice? Or rather, how could she design her life so that all of her passions were honored? The answer for Charlie, or for you, cannot simply be "follow your passion." It must be "follow your passion" plus something else. And this "something else" must tell you how to channel *all* of your passions in a productive, healthy way.

How about setting clearer goals? Well, neither Anna's nor Charlie's life could be said to be driven by a specific goal or dream—Anna never said, "I've gotta get out of Iowa and head to Tinseltown!" She just sort of ended up there. Of course, that doesn't necessarily mean that dreams are without value. I'm sure you have dreams. You don't know if you will ever achieve these dreams, but you hold on to them tightly, and they give you focus, a bright, clear beacon whether your life is storm-tossed or at a standstill.

Yet you mustn't entrust your life to dreams because, unfortunately, all the research we have on dreams and goals reveals that we are woefully inaccurate at predicting which dreams will fulfill us. Money is the simplest example. Many of us yearn to earn more money, and we make many decisions in our lives based on increasing our earning power. But the jury is in on the link between money and happiness. If you live in poverty, you will be less happy than those who live above the poverty line; however, once above the poverty line, you do not become happier the more money you make. So by all means, hold your dreams of a bigger house and a healthier bank account close to your heart, but don't imagine that either one will necessarily make you happier.

And even if one of your wildest dreams comes true, you are wired, as are all human beings, to become hardened to the joys of this dream, just as you are wired to become increasingly immune to the sadness of a tragedy. A famous series of experiments compared the satisfaction levels of lottery winners just after they'd won the lottery with paraplegics' satisfaction levels just after the accident that paralyzed them. Initially, as you'd expect, the lottery winners' satisfaction rose and the paraplegics' sank, but then, after only six months, each person's daily level of satisfaction returned to the level it was before. How trustworthy can dreams be if a happy fantasy and a terrible nightmare leave you, after six months, feeling the same as you did before?

I'm not saying you shouldn't have goals and dreams. Merely that if you target your entire life toward attaining a particular goal or dream, you may well find that it doesn't leave you feeling quite as fulfilled as you had hoped.

There's one other difference we might consider, a slight variation on the one above. Could it be the power of intention? That Anna had it, and Charlie didn't? You could certainly make the case that the Annas of the world launch more positive thoughts out into the universe than the Charlies, and that these thoughts then become reality; that the Annas actually create their futures by believing more deliberately and visualizing more vividly the strong lives they want. And it would be quite a convincing case—Anna's life did indeed become stronger at the very moment when her projections into the future became more vivid: "I am intrigued by the details of the deals in the entertainment industry. So I should seek out work where I am involved with these details."

However, this emphasis on intention raises an even more intriguing conundrum.

Anna's intentions sprung from the Anna-like voice inside her head that was telling her what to do. But why should she trust this voice? How did she know that what it was telling her to do would actually fulfill her? Charlie heard this voice, too, and her intentions were equally vivid: "I see myself married to Peter, working with Peter, moving out of our sketchy neighborhood, and playing with my kids in our front yard." And all these vivid intentions came true.

And yet they broke her down completely.

There is, it seems, such a thing as a trustworthy intention and an untrustworthy intention. They both sound the same in your head, but one leads to fulfillment while the other leads to emptiness. The practice of living a strong life must help you create the former and avoid the latter.

So, if the difference between the Annas of the world and the Charlies isn't drive, a caring partner, or pure passion, and if both goals and intentions can *misguide* as easily as guide, where does this leave you? What can you do to ensure that you strike out on the right path and that, on your journey, you gain the strength you need to stay on this path?

WHAT TO TAKE AWAY FROM THIS CHAPTER

- Two people with similar levels of education, health, similar marital and family status, can still wind up with drastically different feelings of well-being and life satisfaction.
- Though married people tend to be happier than those who are single, or divorced, a loving partner does not necessarily lead you toward the right choices for you and your life.
- Passion is a vital ingredient in living a strong life, but it is by no means the only ingredient. Most often the key challenge of life is not finding your passion, but knowing how to integrate many passions into one life.
- While having clear goals can help you live a strong life, neither having goals, nor attaining those goals is enough to sustain you throughout your life. There is evidence that we soon adapt to the attainment of a goal and quickly feel the ache for something more. More often than not, your attainments fuel, rather than quench, your aspirations.
- Some intentions are trustworthy and should be closely attended to and acted on. Some are untrustworthy and should be ignored. Wisdom lies in knowing the difference.

6

CATCH-AND-CRADLE

How can you call upon life to strengthen you?

The greater part of our happiness or misery depends
on our disposition and not on our circumstances.

—MARTHA WASHINGTON (1731–1802), American First Lady

The secret to living a strong life is not hidden from you. It is not cached in some recessed corner of your personality. It is not "out there" somewhere in the future, in some perfect job you have yet to find or some goal you have yet to reach. Nor is it a random thing, tossed around haphazardly by the fates.

The secret to living a strong life is right in front of you, calling to you every day. It can be found in your emotional reaction to specific moments in your life.

How to Be True to Yourself

Certain moments in your life create in you strongly positive emotions—let's call these "strong-moments." Not all moments are strong-moments—some moments spark negative emotions, while some don't spark any emotions at all. But when you do experience a strong-moment, it is authentic. It is *true*, in the sense that the emotions you feel are true. You may not know exactly what you should do with your emotions, or what label you should give each emotion, but you know how a specific moment made you *feel*. You know if the moment conjured within you a strongly positive *feeling*. You know this more certainly than you know virtually anything else in your life.

Pick an aspect of your life—work perhaps, or your kids, or your spouse—and now picture in your mind's eye a specific highlight moment from last week. (I don't mean an instant. Think of a strong-moment as an event. It might last ten minutes or three hours, but it always has a beginning and an end.) Imagine the details of the moment: What were you actually doing—were you walking, sitting, listening, thinking? Where were you—outside, in your favorite room in your house, in the shower, driving, on the phone? Who was with you—a colleague at work, one of your kids, or were you alone? Put yourself right back into the vivid detail of the moment.

Are you there?

I don't know what you are picturing right now. It could be that moment yesterday when, as you sat hunched over the year-end results, you found a revealing pattern in the financial report you were reading; or the snuggling of your grandson into the crook of your shoulder as you read him the last chapter of *The Magic Treehouse*; or that glorious sentence you wrote last night on your blog; or the way you managed to calm down your colleague after your boss changed everyone's schedule.

For Charlie, it might be the forty-five minutes of silence between her and her husband as they filled two backpacks for their weekend camping trip. For Anna, it might be the conference call she set up between a producer fascinated by the psychology of deception and a writer she'd found who was researching a book on the same subject.

Whatever *you* are picturing, it will be a vivid, detailed moment, and as you think about it now, you feel yourself change. You are sitting up a little straighter than you were even a minute ago. Your shoulders are back. You've slowed down your breathing just a hair. Perhaps you are smiling. This moment, and the emotions you feel as you relive it in your mind, is you, in truth.

When you commit your life to being true to yourself, you are not committing to some far-flung destiny, some grand dream, or some disembodied list of values, no matter how worthy. Instead you are committing to the truth embodied in this strong-moment, the truth that this specific moment, for no rational reason, energizes you.

Back to Anna and Charlie. We could debate for hours what the "right" decisions were for Charlie, but what we can't debate is that she went to Barnes and Noble to buy books on systems integration or that designing the grief counseling sessions at her daughter's school fulfilled her. These strong-moments are her truth.

We could question whether it was fair for Anna's husband to stay home while she worked, but we can't question that she found herself picking up a pair of scissors, snipping articles, storing them in boxes, and then transporting them halfway around the world. The emotional reaction to do this is part of her truth.

Both Anna and Charlie can find in their daily lives many specific strong-moments, many moments when they feel a strongly positive emotional reaction, a reaction they know is true, a reaction they can trust as authentic. As can you. As can we all. The fundamental difference between Anna and Charlie when we first met them, though, was that Anna took her strong-moments seriously and used them to guide her choices and energize her journey; whereas Charlie, for many reasons—some quite noble—did not.

If you want your life to follow an Anna-like trajectory, or, if you feel your life sliding away from you in the same way that Charlie's did, you must do as Anna did: pick out the specific strong-moments in each aspect of your life and then allow them to work their guiding, energizing magic.

Of course, that's a lot easier to write than it is to do. There are days when it's hard to believe that there are any strong-moments out there at all. *Life's moments can strengthen me? Yeah, right!* you think to yourself in the frantic moments of a Monday morning when you're hunting for your daughter's socks, she hasn't brushed her hair like you asked, your son thinks he left his homework in his cubby at school but he can't remember and would you please come upstairs and look for it under his bed, and your husband is sidling out the front door doing his best impression of someone who has terribly important things to say into his cell phone.

Or on a Thursday evening in the kids' bedroom, in the presleep hushing and hair stroking and soothing, when you whisper that you "have to do a *big* presentation next week because Mommy just got this awesome promotion at work. And isn't it great? 'Yea, Mommy!' And good night, sweet dreams. And oh, maybe I might not be able to be there for the Christmas carol sing-a-long." And, suddenly, any thoughts of sleep vanish, and the tears come, and the desperate drama, and the inevitable truth-telling, "But Mommy, every other mommy will be there."

Or when you grab the phone on your way out the door and some official voice tells you that your daughter's best friend, the one whom she stands up for when the bullies at school start in with their teasing, the one whom she forgot to call back last night, committed suicide at eight o'clock this morning.

At times like these you can be forgiven for thinking that the moments of life are less a source of strength than a burden to be borne, a relentless piling on of mishaps, misunderstandings, and misery. Yes, at these times life seems like a pass-fail test where mere survival is success—it can make you stronger, but only because you didn't let it break you.

The strong-life practice—to contrast it with juggling, we can call it the catch-and-cradle practice—asks you to take a different view of life. It doesn't deny that life can be challenging, confusing, even overwhelming. But it asks you to have faith that hidden within life's daily blizzard of moments are some specific moments that can energize you, and that you are both perceptive enough to identify them and powerful enough to push your life toward them.

Catch

Believing that moments in life can strengthen you is not the same as simply having a positive attitude. The practice of catching-and-cradling is not merely positive thinking. Yes, it requires you to be optimistic, but yours must be a *targeted* optimism. The kind of optimism that gives you faith that these strong-moments are out there, and, at the same time, admits that there are many other moments out there that will weaken you. When you catch something, you are focused. You move toward the target, reach for it, grasp it, and then draw it into your body. You are selective.

This was one of the key differences between Charlie and Anna. Charlie was a positive thinker who tended to look on the bright side of every situation, and this positivity was undoubtedly a blessing—not least because it helped her offer meaningful support to those who were suffering. And yet it also led her astray. It led her to the belief that she could twist every moment around in her mind and reconstitute it so that it strengthened her.

You can't do this. You must face up to the fact that some moments have negative energy for you. They are emotionally draining. Trying to put a positive charge on these weak moments is, at best, a short-term survival strategy: it may help you get through the day, but, over time, it will hollow out your life.

Anna seemed to realize this instinctively. She approached life as a *seeker*, as someone who was hunting for strong-moments in her life, who was deeply optimistic that she would find them, and, at the same time, was dismissive of those moments that drained her—that's why she left Iowa, and why she quit her *COPS* job even though she had no alternative career plan. She took her search very seriously, and when she didn't find what she was looking for, she moved on quickly, and with little regret. She was still searching.

Study strong lives closely and you will discover this same kind of targeted optimism, this same active searching for strong-moments. These people are not just "living in the moment." They are "searching *for* the moment." To live a strong life, you must do the same. You must become a seeker, always looking for specific moments to catch.

No one else can do this for you, because your strong-moments are not the same as anyone else's. Anna clipped and clipped and clipped for no good reason other than her love of information. Charlie bought systems integration books and tried to visualize what the perfect configuration of moving parts would be.

I imagine that, on some level, you know this instinctively. You know that the strategy of mimicking another person's approach to life will never serve you. That's why so much advice from well-intentioned people in your life, loud and persuasive though it may be, actually goes unheeded; or, if it's heeded, isn't implemented very well. You sense that what works for them won't work for you—that while they adore going on school field trips with the kids, you shuffle off the school bus swearing to yourself that you will feign an injury before you again volunteer to chaperone twenty nine-year-olds at the museum; or that while they advise you to relax by sitting in front of your favorite TV show with a glass of wine, you know that, strange as it sounds, rearranging your desk or labeling your family photos is far more relaxing. You sense that the only person who can legitimately recognize your strong-moments for what they are is the person who sees what you see, notices what you notice, feels what you feel, loves what you love. You.

Cradle

Your unique personality determines which moments strengthen you. And it's true that no matter how much you may want to change your-self, the basic shape of your personality remains remarkably stable throughout the course of your life. For example, even if they wanted to (which they don't), Charlie will never learn to shut off her craving for a better way of arranging things, and Anna will never quell her yearning for more information.

However, what *can* happen, and often does, is you can stop paying attention to the moments that strengthen you. You can stop listening to them, striving to create more of them, and celebrating them. And when you stop, the emotional signals fade and fade, until, eventually, the connection breaks and the signals die. Neglect is a strength-killer.

This is, in part, what happened to Charlie. She stopped paying attention to the specific moments in her life that strengthened her and instead allowed herself to be borne along by other people's needs. For example, she was strengthened by designing systems, not by running these systems. But she didn't notice this distinction. She didn't appreciate it. Indeed, it's fair to say, she didn't truly understand it. And so when circumstances conspired to pull her away into a different world, a world with fewer of these strengthening moments, she unwittingly sacrificed what she never knew she needed.

You know people who do the same. They stop paying attention to which moments strengthen them, and, disconnected from the specifics of who they are and what they need, they allow their lives to be led by other people's wants. And just like that, they slide into a harmful life-pattern, a self-reinforcing downward spiral that is as devastating as it is commonplace. If and when (and I hope it's "if") this downward spiral occurs in your life, it will look something like this:

Because you neglect the specific moments that strengthen you, your life gradually becomes filled up with a grab bag of activities and responsibilities. You might have a good reason for taking on each of these responsibilities—everything from "If I don't do this, no one else will" to "A good mother *should* do this"—but the outcome is that the barrage of moments with which you've filled your life now blankets your senses. This barrage drowns out the signals from those few moments that do truly strengthen you. You start to feel empty.

Aware of these feelings of emptiness but unaware of their source, you take on yet more responsibilities in the hope that by doing more, you will feel more. (When I met Charlie, she was not only running the office and the family, she was also the treasurer of one local society and sat on the board of two others.)

These new responsibilities further overwhelm your senses. Moment by moment, you feel not more, but less—less resilient, less fulfilled, less strong.

And as you feel yourself weaken, you become confused. You start to think that the problem is that you haven't managed your time properly, that if you could just get more structure into your life, be more organized, put up proper boundaries, learn to say no, and shut off the computer, you wouldn't feel quite so overwhelmed.

But no matter how firm your boundaries are, you still feel empty because the moments inside those boundaries don't strengthen you.

This perpetual state of feeling overwhelmed wears you down, and little pricks of panic surprise you, and then swell into full-blooded life-fears: "What am I doing wrong? Where will this lead?" These questions become louder, drowning out the few strong signals life is still sending you . . .

Down the spiral twists, with your days filling up and your life emptying out.

Sorry not to sound more cheery, but this spiral is real and it's destructive and it happens all too frequently. Of the thirty women participating in my Career Intervention workshop, more than half of them had fallen into it. They weren't suffering because they were living a second-rate version of somebody else's life. Rather they had stopped paying attention to the strong-moments in their lives and so were living a second-rate version of their own.

This spiral ends in real psychological (and sometimes physiological) pain, but it starts with just a few neglected moments. Don't let this happen to you.

Instead, once you've caught the strong-moments in your life, *cradle* them.

Cradling isn't merely holding. Cradling is a careful and creative action.

- *When you cradle something, you concentrate on it.* Cradling means paying attention. It means looking at the moment from new angles and delighting in the details you discover.
- *When you cradle something, you accept it.* You feel its weight and allow it to move you. Cradling creates imbalance, which, in turn, creates direction. It leads, and you follow.
- *When you cradle something, you nurture it.* Your hand isn't closed like a fist. It is cupped, protective of what it's holding, but also open to the possibility of growth. When you cradle something, you are hopeful.

So when you are trying to decide what to do with your career, cradle your strongest moments and let them guide you. When you are trying to make peace between competing responsibilities in your life, accept what these moments tell you and allow them to set your priorities.

When life's mishaps have set you back and all you see is darkness, pay close attention to your strongest moments and they will lift you up and show you the first glimmers of light.

There's more to it than this, of course. How can you identify these moments? What about your many other responsibilities? What about delayed gratification and making sacrifices for a better future? We'll deal with these issues later in the book. For now, know this: The secret to living a strong life is to catch the strongest moments in each part of your life and cradle them.

The "Catch-and-Cradle" Practice Made Simple

Search for Strong-Moments

Life persists in distracting you with a dizzying array of energetic signals—careers you could pursue, life choices you could make, people you could get close to, moments you could re-create. Hidden within this array are the few signals that truly invigorate you—careers you *should* pursue, life choices you *should* make, people you *should* get close to, moments you *should* re-create. How can you sort it all out?

Attend to your emotions. Your emotions are the signals life sends you. Stop *transmitting*—quiet your goals, plans, claims, and intentions—and start *receiving* these signals. They will guide you to make the right choices. On the flip side, if you are inattentive to these emotional signals, not only will you make poor choices, but over time these signals will fade, and you'll disconnect from yourself.

To help you, take the Strong Life test, provided in chapter 7. This test measures you against the nine positive roles we all play in life and reveals which role you are born to play. Your results will help

You must learn how to choose, how to focus your life toward specific moments. You must learn how to create more of the strong-moments you want and how to celebrate the ones you have. Yours will not be a balanced life—as we'll see, balance is both impossible to maintain and unfulfilling on those few occasions when you do strike it. But if you learn to create and celebrate your strong-moments, yours will be a full life, inclined, tilted, targeted toward your strongest moments. So often you are told: "You must learn to say 'No.'" But, to live your strongest life, you must do the opposite. You must learn to say 'Yes.' Yes, to the strong moments in each part of your life. Yes, to the people who help you create these moments. Yes, to your feelings as these moments happen. Say 'Yes' with enough focus and force, and you'll have little need for 'no.'

In the next three chapters, we will dive into each of these parts of the practice. You'll take a test that will reveal the role you were born to play; you'll meet women who've accepted where their strong-moments led them and who've been lifted up by these moments; and you'll learn how to take control of your life, imbalance it, and connect to the strength you need.

WHAT TO TAKE AWAY FROM THIS CHAPTER

○ **Moments matter most.** They matter more than dreams, goals, values or relationships. Moments makes all these other things real.

○ **For no good reason other than the nature of your personality, certain moments create in you strong positive feelings.** In these strong-moments you will find your truth.

○ **The happiest and most successful women identify these specific moments in each aspect of their life, and actively seek them out.**

○ **They are optimistic.** They are not so optimistic as to believe that every moment can be made to strengthen them. But, in each aspect of their life, they actively seek out these strong-moments, and they are predisposed to believe that they will find what they are looking for.

○ **Once they have found their strong-moments, they pay deliberate attention to them.** They realize that, since attention amplifies everything, the more they focus on these strong-moments the more vivid, powerful and energizing these moments become.

○ **The better they concentrate on these strong-moments, the better they feel about letting other moments fall away.**

○ **This habit of seeking out strong moments and paying close attention to them can be called "Catching-and Cradling."** It is the life-long practice of the happiest and most successful women.

7

SEARCH FOR STRONG-MOMENTS

Which role were you born to play?

Success is liking yourself, liking what you do,
and liking how you do it.

—MAYA ANGELOU (b. 1928), author and poet

H ow often do we stop paying attention to people because we assume we know them? We see what they're wearing, how they're talking, the company they're keeping, and we draw our conclusions. We finish their story for them. We fill in their blanks. And because we stop asking questions, we never really get to know them. We may come to tolerate them. But tolerance is a cop-out. Tolerance is about distance, keeping things separate and putting up with them. It's not about listening. It's not about being inquisitive. Though we may tolerate them, we never come to see the world fully through their eyes. And so we can't empathize with them. We can't respect them. We can't love them. We can't take a stand for them.

And who is the first person who suffers from our tolerance? Who is the first person we make assumptions about, whose circumstances we put up with, whom we keep at a safe distance, whom we struggle to empathize with, to respect, to love, truly? Who is the first person for whom we fail to take a stand? Ourselves.

It's so easy to slip into a role we assume is right for us. It feels comfortable, inevitable, even virtuous. We say things like:

- "Of course I must keep working full-time, because our family needs the health-care benefits."
- "Of course I must continue with my residency, because my mother and father have already spent so much money on my education. I can't throw all that away."
- "Of course I must quit working and look after the kids. After all, what can be more important than my kids?"

Any one of these roles may turn out to be the one for you to play, but whatever you decide to do with your life, don't base your decision on what you *assume* is the right role for you to play. Base your decision on the fact that you value yourself enough to be inquisitive, to ask the questions, and to listen closely to what your emotions are telling you. Only then will you find the moments that strengthen you. Only then will you discover the role you were born to play.

Research reveals that women are more likely to attribute their success to external factors, such as luck or other people, whereas men tie their success to internal factors, such as their own strengths. Undoubtedly, this gives men more self-assurance when tackling the next challenge, asking for that promotion, or negotiating for that raise. Dig into the research more deeply, however, and you discover that not all women are the same. The most successful women, as measured by level of professional achievement, (not the perfect metric, I know) think more like men. They explain their success by pointing to their own strengths and by describing how they channeled these strengths toward outstanding performance.

To help you pinpoint your own strengths, take the Strong Life Test. You can find it at StrongLifeTest.com. I encourage you to pass it on to anyone who you think could benefit from more focus and clarity in her life.

The Strong Life Test:
Discover the Role You Were Born to Play

Though I've worked on many talent profiles over the last two decades, the most well known is the StrengthsFinder profile, developed with Dr. Donald Clifton. When Don and I originally designed StrengthsFinder—he identified the questions, while I wrote the descriptions of the thirty-four talent themes the test measures—our goal was to split up the many different aspects of your personality and present you with your top five themes of talent. We wanted to give you, and the rest of the world, a common language to describe all that is right with you. At the time, this was a novel idea; most psychological profiles were built to measure what was wrong with you. But in the last few years, it has proven so popular that each year more than a million people around the world complete it.

The purpose of the Strong Life test is different. Rather than splitting apart all the different aspects of you, the Strong Life test puts you back together. It measures you against nine life roles and reveals which role is your Lead Role. (It will also show you your second strongest role, your Supporting Role.)

These nine life roles were derived from my analysis of personality test results over the last two decades. When you look closely at thousands of results, you discover that, although each one of us is endlessly unique, certain repeating patterns always emerge. These patterns aren't sterile "factors" or "types." Rather they are emotional. These patterns cause you to feel love and joy and fear and pain. They give you great patience in some parts of your life, and intense impatience elsewhere. They draw you toward certain kinds of people, while repelling you from others. They color your dreams and shape your desire. They are, in Professor James Hillman's lovely phrase, your "soul's code."

Because, in the end, they define your character, I chose to call them Life Roles. There are nine:

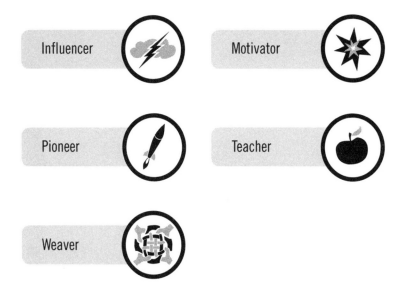

In the Strong Life test, my colleague, Dr. Courtney McCashland, and I present you with a number of scenarios and then challenge you to identify which decision you would make. As with all such tests, the results will be most accurate when you take it with an unprepared mind, so I'd advise you to go online and complete it before you read the descriptions on the following pages. And when you do take it, be sure to go with your top-of-mind response; your immediate, unfiltered reaction is always the most revealing.

Of course, your test results will not define you completely—there's a good deal more fine-tuning you'll want to do on your own to add detail and specificity. But what the test will do is show you where to start your search for a strong life.

On the following pages are the descriptions of these roles, along with suggestions of how to make the most of your Lead and Supporting Roles.

ADVISOR

You begin by asking, *"What is the best thing to do?"* and your thrill comes from knowing that you are the person others turn to for the answer. You don't necessarily want to be the person who actually makes the changes happen. Rather, what excites you is being valued by others for your insight and your judgment. Since you love to be the expert, you are constantly on the lookout for information that will help people make better decisions. When you look out at the world, you pay attention to fine shadings of detail because these details will ensure that you give better advice. You know that the best advice is never general, but rather is tailored to the unique characteristics of the person or the situation. You can be demanding and opinionated, but above all you are discriminating: "good enough" is never good enough for you. There is always a better way, a better arrangement, a better solution, and you come alive when you are called upon to find it. And when you do, you don't question your decision. The reason people seek you out for guidance is precisely because you are so assured, so confident in your intuition. Instinctively you know this, and you're proud of it.

You know you are an Advisor if:

- You ask lots of questions.
- You are impatient for things to get done.
- You take pleasure in fine distinctions.
- You are always explaining things.
- You trust your gut.

Your strongest moments are when:

- You discover the few critical improvements that make the difference.
- Someone calls you up out of the blue and relies on your opinion.
- You clarify a complex issue for someone, she acts on what you told her, and you see her succeed.
- You land on a distinction that reveals an elemental truth about the world.
- You are asked to be an expert witness.

To make the most of your role:

- Do your homework. Friends and colleagues will come to you because you trust your judgment, so make sure you inform your judgment with facts.
- Build your bank of distinctions. Practice the words, phrases, or examples that will bring clarity to a situation.
- Learn to tailor your advice to the person. The success of your advice will depend not only on how wise it is but also on how easy it is for the other person to comprehend it and put it into action.
- Learn to hide your impatience. Some people will never understand the distinctions you are making, no matter how carefully you tailor your advice. When you meet such people, don't become dismissive—if you do, you will quickly gain a reputation as a know-it-all, and this reputation will make people question how safe it is to ask your advice. And if people stop coming to you for advice, you won't have the chance to be an Advisor. So, instead of being dismissive, simply stop advising her and figure out a polite way to move on to someone who can understand what you are saying.
- When you find yourself in a management role, be sure to surround yourself with action-oriented people. You are a natural delegator, and this is all well and good so long as the people around you have the talent required to understand and execute your advice. Rather than complaining about the lack of talent around you, take it upon yourself to seek out people who love to make things happen. They will complement and amplify your advice. They'll make you look good.

CARETAKER

You begin by asking, *"Is everyone okay?"* You are acutely aware of others' emotional states, particularly if you sense they are feeling hurt or slighted. You are instinctively inclusive, always looking for ways to draw others into the circle and make them feel wanted, heard, and appreciated. You pay close attention to the differences between people, each person's likes, dislikes, and foibles. It's the only way to attend to their feelings, you think. You are protective of other people and will get angry or upset if you see behavior that is cavalier or dismissive of people's feelings. You are an intensely loyal and forgiving friend, but you are no pushover. Although your circle is large, it does have a perimeter, and if someone's behavior offends you, you will exile them beyond the perimeter. This will pain you, but you will do it anyway. At home and work, many will come to trust you and rely on you: you are their safe harbor, a consistently supportive presence in a world that doesn't care. And they love you for it.

You know you are a Caretaker if:

- You want others to like you and you work to make them like you. You are good at it, and it gives you strength.
- You pay attention to each person's idiosyncrasies.
- You check in with people frequently.
- You build a large circle of friends—not acquaintances, but true friends, people you know well and care about deeply.
- You create passionate loyalty in others.

Your strongest moments are when:

- People confide in you.
- Your friends come to you over others.

- You anticipate what someone else will love and get it right.
- You relieve others' stress.
- You find a productive way to include someone who has been left out.

To make the most of your role:

- Learn to use the goodwill you create. Yes, you are a Caregiver because you can't help it. But that doesn't mean you can't ask for anything in return. While your support is virtually unconditional, the fact that you were there to provide it will cause others to want to do things for you. Take responsibility for channeling this goodwill toward an important, valuable goal. A Caregiver is a powerful role in that you create willingness in others. Learn to use it.
- Figure out how technology can help you. For example, social networking sites such as Facebook, Twitter, and MySpace can both maintain and expand your circle by providing you with up-to-date news of each person's likes, successes, and feelings.
- Find distinct moments of joy in this role. The danger of this role is that you allow yourself to become consumed by the other person's feelings and forget your own. To avoid this danger, don't fight your Caregiver role—you'll never shake it. Instead learn to locate your own satisfaction in how the other person comes to view you. You will never be able to control her feelings (and you'll torture yourself if you try), but you can control what you say to her and do for her, and so you can control how she comes to see you. Locate your joy in how she sees you—a consistently supportive presence.
- Define the perimeter of your circle. What behavior would move someone beyond that perimeter? If someone did something unethical, would you still be there to support her? If she borrowed money from you and failed to repay it, would you still support her? If she hurt another person, would you still be there for her? Draw the line of your perimeter, and it will be much less tormenting (though never easy) on those few occasions when you need to exile someone beyond it.

CREATOR

You begin by asking, *"What do I understand?"* You aren't immune to the feelings and perspectives of others, but your starting point is your own insight, your own understanding. You see the world as a series of collisions between competing parts, pieces, and agendas; and you are compelled to figure it all out. For you there's nothing quite as thrilling as finding a pattern beneath life's craziness, a core concept that can explain why things play out the way they do, or better yet, predict how things are going to play out. You are a thoughtful person, someone who needs time alone to mull and muse and percolate. Without this alone time, events pile up on you haphazardly, and your confusion starts to overwhelm you. So you look forward to time by yourself—early in the morning, late at night, long flights—and you use this time to get clear. You are a creative person. What form this creativity takes will depend on your other traits and talents, but whether you write, paint, sing, complete projects, or make presentations, you are drawn toward making things. Each thing you make is a tangible sign that you have made some sense of the world, that you have organized the chaos in some useful way. You look at what you've made, you take pleasure in what you now understand, and then you move on to the next creation.

You know you're a Creator if:

- ○ You feel uncomfortable if a day goes by without producing some tangible sign of insight or understanding.
- ○ You push yourself hard, rarely stopping to celebrate your accomplishments. There's still so much left to make sense of.
- ○ You read a lot of nonfiction.

- You are inspired by the achievements of others—not their growth and development, necessarily, but what they have achieved. You are more interested in destinations than journeys.

Your strongest moments are when:

- You figure something out.
- You spend time by yourself reading, writing, preparing your mind.
- A fresh insight dawns on you.
- You have an in-depth conversation with someone.
- You get a chance to show your expertise.

To make the most of your role:

- Take time to celebrate what you've achieved. It will inspire you to keep creating.
- Explain to others that you are at your best when you have time to think things through, that you're not good at making snap decisions. Without this explanation, people may come to see you as indecisive.
- Deliberately involve other people—friends, colleagues, family—in helping you think things through. It will make them feel involved, and it will stop you from going around and around in circles in your head—which you sometimes find yourself doing.
- Carry a notebook around with you. Insights pop up at inopportune moments, and you will want to have a place to capture them.

EQUALIZER

You begin by asking, *"What's the right thing to do?"* You are sensitive to how everything in the world is connected, how movement in one part of the world causes everything else to move as well. Alive to this interconnectedness, you feel compelled to keep everything aligned. This need for alignment might be organizational—you sense when your world is disorganized and you get a kick out of restoring everything to its rightful place. Or it might be ethical—you are acutely aware of who is responsible for what, and you are quick to take action if someone doesn't live up to her responsibilities. You have no problem calling her out if she hasn't followed through, and you are just as willing to call yourself out when you drop the ball. You see the commitments we make to one another as threads that connect us and allow us to share in each other's success. It pains you when you see these threads break, and so you are their passionate protector. At your best, you are our conscience, helping us realize how much we owe one another and how much we rely on one another. You hold us together.

You know you are an Equalizer if:

- You do best when deadlines and time frames are clear.
- You spend a lot of time defining the rules of the game.
- You become an ardent and active supporter of the causes you commit to.
- You stand up for what is right even when it is not popular to do so.

Your strongest moments are when:

- You make things right when someone has been wronged.
- You defend a person or principle in the face of resistance.
- You get things organized.
- You clarify the rules we should all be playing by.
- Others ask you to render a judgment and then do what you say.

To make the most of your role:

- Seek out situations that are messy and beg for structure. You are one of the few who actually gets a kick out of imposing a grid on the world; so the rest of us will rely heavily on you in chaotic situations.
- Lead with your values. Find a non–self-righteous way to tell people what your core values are. Your values make you predictable, and this predictability will cause people to trust you.
- Learn to draw a distinction between your core values—which you will never change—and the other parts of life where you are happy to entertain a different perspective or a new way of doing things. This way others will not mistake your unchanging core for rigidity.
- Choose carefully who and what you are going to defend. You are an ardent defender of those whom you think have been wronged, including yourself. This is an admirable trait, but it can sometimes be seen as all-too-frequent defensiveness.

INFLUENCER

You begin by asking, *"How can I move you to act?"* In virtually every situation, your eye goes to the outcome. Whether you are in a long meeting at work, helping one of your kids do her homework, or talking a friend off a ledge, you measure your success by your ability to persuade the other person to do something she didn't necessarily intend to do. You may do this by the force of your arguments, your charm, or your ability to outwit her, or perhaps by some combination of all of these, but, regardless of your method, what really matters to you is moving the other person to action. Why? Partly because you see where things will lead if the other person doesn't act, and partly because you are instinctively aware of momentum and so become frustrated when you bump into someone who slows down your momentum. But mostly because you just can't help it. It's simply fun for you to influence people's behavior through the power of your personality. It's challenging and mysterious and thrilling, and, in the end, of course, it makes good things happen.

You know you are an Influencer if:

- You enjoy closing the sale.
- You sometimes challenge people more than you should.
- You are someone others rely on to say it like it is.
- You enjoy a little resistance to your ideas because it gives you a chance to show just how persuasive you can be.

Your strongest moments are when:

- You find the right lever to move someone to action.
- You make someone think that your idea is theirs.
- You bargain with someone and wind up with a great deal.
- You are called on to make the final decision.
- You are on the front lines, moving things forward.

To make the most of your role:

- Seek out situations with inherent resistance—such as sales or fund-raising—and your value will be immediately apparent to everyone. Many people are intimidated by resistance and try to avoid it. You aren't. You are at your best when trying to push through resistance and keep the momentum going.
- Listen closely for other people's "hot buttons." These are key to moving them to action. The faster you can identify them, the faster you'll get things moving.
- Be discriminating. When you are confronted with group resistance, find the decision maker. Don't waste your Influencer role on someone who can't make things happen.
- Ignore people who tell you to be patient. Instead, if progress is slow in coming, look for small wins along the way that can satisfy your need for momentum.

MOTIVATOR

You begin by asking, *"How can I raise the energy?"* You are acutely aware of the energy in the room, and you feel compelled to do what you can to elevate it. You do this with your outlook—you are an instinctively optimistic person. You do this with your actions—you take a seat at the front of the room, you raise your hand to ask questions, you call upon others to contribute and volunteer. You do this with your humor—the smile in your voice. Because you are an energy-giving person, other people are attracted to you. The world beats them down, but they know that in you they will find the power to lift themselves back up. You aren't soft and gentle. On the contrary, you challenge people to unleash their own energy, and you become impatient when someone refuses to do so, sucking your energy from you and generating none of her own. But, still, others will continue to be drawn to you because they sense that, at heart, you cannot help but be encouraging. They sense that your natural reaction is to celebrate all that is good in them, to illuminate their strengths, and to shine a light on their achievements. Even on your darkest days, you know they are right.

You know you're a Motivator if:

- You have more social requests than you know what to do with.
- You have an infectious laugh.
- You love throwing parties for other people, though not necessarily for yourself. (You get a kick out of shining a spotlight on other people rather than yourself.)
- You are sought out, and worn out, by emotional vampires.
- You collect inspirational stories and quotes.

Your strongest moments are when:

- You laugh—and also when you cry.
- You make others laugh.
- You are told, "You're an inspiration to me."
- You are able to take charge of a group and raise their spirits.
- You plan a celebration for someone and see her reaction.

To make the most of your role:

- Figure out whether you are best at motivating people who are deeply unmotivated, or people who are doing just fine and who need a jolt to take them to the next level. These are distinct versions of this role, and it is unlikely that you are invigorated by both.
- Study what works. When you have been extraordinarily effective at elevating people to new heights, take the time to figure out why. What exactly did you do that worked so well?
- Learn the best way to extricate yourself from people who want to feed off your energy but who offer little in return. If you're not careful, these people will deplete you.
- Figure out which specific activities recharge your own energy levels. As a Motivator, you will be forever pouring your energy into others. This is a wonderful role, but only if you know how to fill yourself back up.

PIONEER

You begin by asking, *"What's new?"* You are, by nature, an explorer, excited by things you haven't seen before, people you haven't yet met. Whereas others are intimidated by the unfamiliar, you are intrigued by it. It fires your curiosity and heightens your senses—you are smarter and more perceptive when you're doing something you've never done before. With ambiguity comes risk, and you welcome this. Instinctively you know you are a resourceful person, and since you enjoy calling upon this aspect of yourself, you actively seek out situations where there is no beaten path, where it's up to you to figure out how to keep moving forward. You sense that your appetite for the unknown might be an attempt to fill a void, and some days you wonder what you are trying to prove to yourself. But mostly you leave the questioning and the analyzing to others and revel in your pioneering nature. You are at your best when you ask a question no one has asked, try a technique no one has tried, feel an experience few have felt. We need you at your best. You lead us into the undiscovered country.

You know you are a Pioneer if:

- You are quickly bored.
- You are always thinking about new business ideas.
- You are excitable and curious.
- You don't read instructions.
- You are an early adopter of new technology.

Your strongest moments are when:

- You're starting something new.
- Your plans change suddenly and you have to improvise.
- You push yourself beyond your limits.
- You're talking about what's next.
- You're not quite sure what's about to happen.

To make the most of your role:

- Seek out experts. They will help you look around the corner and prepare you for the challenges you are about to face.
- Look for situations where things become obsolete very quickly. Careers in high-tech, news media, fashion, and applied research will naturally intrigue you because what exists is always about to be replaced with something new.
- Learn how to describe the unknown in vivid detail. The unknown excites you, but it makes others anxious, and you need to turn their anxiety into confidence. The more vivid your word pictures are, the more motivated they will be to join you on your journey.
- Do not listen to those who tell you not to start until every last detail of the plan is in place. Instead, if you want to add detail to something, add detail to the destination. The more clearly you envision where you are going, the more your natural resourcefulness will serve you along the way. Conversely, if your destination isn't clear, there is a chance your willingness to improvise will lead to unproductive zigzagging.

TEACHER

You begin by asking, *"What can she learn from this?"* Your focus is instinctively toward the other person. Not her feelings, necessarily, but her understanding, her skills, and her performance. You see each person as a work in progress, and you are comfortable with this messiness. You don't expect her to be perfect; in fact, you don't want her to be perfect. You like the messiness of imperfection because you know that out of messiness comes choice and that choice leads to learning. Since you are energized by another person's growth, you look for signs of it. "Where was she last month?" you ask yourself. "What measurable progress have I seen?" You create novel ways to keep track of her performance and celebrate with her when she reaches new heights. You ask her a lot of questions to figure out what she knows and what she doesn't, how she learns best, what is important to her, and what journey she is on. Only then can you join her at the appropriate level and in the appropriate way. Only then can you teach her.

You know you're a Teacher if:

- You never give up on anybody. You are convinced that each person is capable of learning and growing.
- You collect vivid stories of how someone overcame an obstacle or made the leap to a new level of understanding.
- You gather facts, experiences, and objects that you think might, at some point, prove useful to a particular person's growth.
- You become a magnet for highly talented people looking for a mentor.

Your strongest moments are when:

- You find a story, a fact, or an object that you can use to help someone learn.
- You design a way to help a person keep track of her progress.
- You see someone finally "get it."
- You take time to learn something for yourself.
- You see a student use a skill that you taught her.

To make the most of your role:

- Define your own learning routine and then stick to it. Your life can become so busy with other people that you forget to take the time to continue your own learning.
- Keep experimenting with new methods of teaching and new technologies. Stay inquisitive and daring, and so will your students.
- Figure out how to design environments that support growth and development in others. For example, ask yourself, "What would a learning family look like?" or "What would a learning team look like?"
- Cultivate two or more mentor relationships. Always make sure you have something to bring your mentors—some experience, insight, discovery, or question—so that they have something of yours to respond to and build on.
- Seek out opportunities to volunteer with people in your community who could benefit from what you have to teach.

WEAVER

You begin by asking, *"With whom can I connect?"* You see the world as a web of relationships, and you are excited by the prospect of connecting people within your web. Not because they will like each other—though they might—but rather because of what they will create together. Your mantra is "One and one makes three." Or thirty. Or three hundred. On your most optimistic days, you see almost no limit to what people with different strengths and perspectives can create together. You are a naturally inquisitive person, always asking questions about each person's background, experience, and skills. You know instinctively that each person brings something unique and distinct to the table, something, no matter how small, that might prove to be the vital ingredient. In your head, or in your contacts, you store a large network of people whom you've met, learned about, cataloged, and positioned somewhere within this network—each person with a link to at least one other person, and each with an open port for another link to be added. People are drawn to you because you are so obviously passionate about their particular expertise, and because you have so many practical ideas about how their expertise can be combined with others. You enliven and enlarge others' vision of who they are and what they can achieve. You are a connector, a multiplier, weaving people together into the fabric of something much larger and more significant than themselves.

You know you are a Weaver if:

- ◎ You have a large circle of acquaintances.
- ◎ You are never at a loss for whom to call.
- ◎ You are always planning whom you are going to introduce to whom.

- You often cold-call people you've heard or read about in order to connect them with someone you know.
- You ask the people you meet a lot of questions about their interests and experiences.

Your strongest moments are when:

- You find common ground between two people who, on the surface, have little in common.
- You sense you are in the middle of the information flow.
- You link a person in your network with a new piece of information that winds up benefiting her.
- Others turn to you to find the right person to help them.

To make the most of your role:

- Choose an area of focus and develop your expertise within it. You are a catalyst; you speed up the reaction between two elements. And like all catalysts, you must bring certain ingredients to the compound if it is to flourish. Your own expertise will always prove to be an important ingredient.
- Make it clear to the people you are connecting what your motive is. Whether your motive is self-interest or something more altruistic is less important than that the other people know what it is. As a Weaver, you are an intermediary. This is a powerful role, but other people will sometimes wonder what your agenda is. And if they don't know, they won't trust you.
- Embrace your role as a peacemaker. When people don't understand one another, step between them and show each how they can benefit from the other. So many conflicts stem from separation—two parties at a distance, not understanding one another. You can bring people of differing views together.
- Always follow through on the connections you make. It's one thing to bring people together; it's another to keep the pressure on until these two people produce something wonderful. It's up to you to keep the pressure on.

Always Sweat the Small Stuff

Now that you've taken the Strong Life test and seen your results, it's time to dig a little deeper.

As you look at your Lead Role and Supporting Role and consider how these roles bring you strength and satisfaction in life, remember this: always sweat the small stuff. The details of the moment matter. Sure, you will be able to use your Lead and Supporting Roles like a compass; they will guide you toward some of the strongest moments in your life. But a compass is not the actual territory. Look more closely at the contours and the content of your life, and you will discover the unique characteristics you bring to each role.

For example, Charlie's Lead Role is Creator, and her Supporting Role is Caretaker. Without doubt, knowing this will prove helpful to her as she organizes her days and plans her years. However, to find her strongest life, she will need to add more detail to these roles. The Creator in her pushes her to wrap her head around complex systems and arrange them more effectively. All right, but what kinds of systems? What kinds of things does she love to design and to figure out? Does she like doing it alone or as part of a team? Is it fun only in areas in which she is expert, or is the novelty of the system—the fact that she knows little about it—the thing that excites her?

Her Caretaker role asks her to reach out and attend to those who've been left out. All right, but which kind of people? All people? Or only young people? And if caring for young people energizes her the most, does it matter what kind of help they need? She cared for violent sex offenders and it wore her out, so is there a certain sort of young person to whom she's drawn naturally? If so, who?

To make intelligent decisions in her life, Charlie can use her Lead and Supporting Roles as the jumping-off point for a focused look at how she engages with the world.

And so can you. Try it now. Bring to mind one highlight moment from last week where you were clearly playing to your Lead Role. Quiet your mind and focus your attention on this moment more closely. Narrow your vision to one detail you are absolutely certain of, and then slowly widen your lens. Inch out from the center and add more details to your mental picture. What do you see? What do you feel? Can you feel the temperature of the room? Can you feel the texture of the clothes you were wearing? What sounds did you hear? Can you hear them again now?

If you were by yourself in this strong-moment, what expression was on your face? Imagine you'd held up a mirror and looked into your eyes. What would you have seen? And if someone else was with you in your strong-moment, what expression was on her face? Was she looking at you? Or was she glancing away?

What moments came just before it? Were you rushing to be there? Did it catch you by surprise? Or did the moment gradually build up from hours of preparation and concentration, or a long conversation?

And what happened right afterward? Where did this strong-moment lead? Did life flow on, disturbing the moment and leaving nothing behind, or did you find traces of the moment in everything you did in the hours, even days, that followed? How long did this moment really last for you?

As before, I obviously have no idea what you are seeing in your mind's eye, but whatever it is, it's vivid. Pay attention to these details.

They will help you realize exactly what it was in the moment that energized you, and as a result, you'll make stronger decisions about your career and your life.

For example, when Anna (Lead Role: Advisor) was trying to decide what she should do with her life, she did the physical equivalent of what I just asked you to do. She sat with her boxes of clippings, pulled them out one by one, and paid attention to each one. She looked at the contents of the clipping, read it, thought about it, let her mind wander from the article to a memory of where she was when she clipped it and why she might have been interested in it, and then, if no more details emerged, she put the clipping aside and moved on to the next one. Each clipping served as an emotional signal, a pulse of energy, setting off a series of associations in her mind. It was as she was following one of these associations that she arrived at the memory of the magazine stand on her campus. Beginning with this mental scene, she slowly widened her focus, adding detail upon detail—"I used to buy the *Hollywood Reporter* every week. I used to skip to the back of the magazine. I used to love the articles describing how complex deals came together"—until she arrived at her insight: "I am energized by what happens behind the scenes. I should look for work in this area."

This wasn't her destiny. It wasn't a dream she'd had since she was a little girl. It was a career choice pieced together from paying attention to how specific moments made her feel.

In retrospect, her career decision seems inevitable. "Of course, Anna should be a talent agent. She was born to do it!" And from the outside you may look at her and think, *She's so lucky. That job fits her perfectly. How did she find that job?*

But we now know the truth. Anna didn't "find" this perfect job. She built it, using as her building blocks her detailed understanding of a few strong-moments in her life.

Candace Nelson did the same. Candace (Lead Role: Motivator) is the owner of a company called Sprinkles. They make cupcakes. Just cupcakes. Beautiful, fresh, ridiculously tempting cupcakes. Drive past their flagship store on any day, and you'll see a long line out the door. Seriously, any day, any hour, you see this line and think, *Really?! Those thirty people are so desperate for a cupcake at 11:07 a.m. on a Tuesday that they are willing to stand in line for twenty minutes*? But apparently they are. From one store in Los Angeles, Candace now has stores in Newport Beach, Dallas, Scottsdale, and Palo Alto, public shout-outs from many a celebrity, and venture capitalists standing in their own line, offering financing and franchising opportunities.

Building Intentions Out of Strong-Moments

From the outside, Candace looks a lot like Anna. Perfect job, perfect life. How did she find that life? As with Anna, her story is much more interesting from the inside.

Candace didn't become a cook straight out of college. Instead, after graduating from Wesleyan, she joined the corporate finance program of an investment bank. Why? "Hard to say now," she admits. "I wanted to lay the groundwork of my career in the appropriate way? I wanted to do what my father wanted me to do? I wanted to prove to the tough guys in banking that I was smart enough to play their game on their terms? All of the above."

Quite soon, however, she realized she'd made a mistake. "Others had their brains prewired for finances and numbers," she said. "Whereas I would have to study and grind it out." She succeeded, but she admits, "It wasn't how my brain worked." At the end of two grueling years, and despite doing well enough to be able to advance further, Candace knew she had to get out.

This was a time when San Francisco was booming with high-tech and Internet companies. Candace saw an opportunity, so she joined the NBC-backed portal Snap.com in business development. She liked the culture, but something was bothering her. Why was she working in a company when a good number of her friends were setting up their own small companies and finding great success? She was entrepreneurial by temperament. Couldn't she be doing the same? Something was wrong about working in a corporate culture like this and, besides, Snap.com wasn't doing that well. So Candace jumped.

Now what? Candace didn't want to fall into another job that wasn't the right fit but she didn't know what that fit was.

"I took all those basic career tests and got a whole bunch of feedback, but I learned pretty much nothing that would be helpful to finding the right career. I was starting to get worried. Money was running low, and with the dot-com bust, everyone was hightailing it out of San Francisco—to rent a U-Haul trailer you had to get on a month long waiting list!"

One day, Candace was chatting with her mother, asking her what she was like as a kid, and her mom started talking about the times they'd go on trips and how, rather than go to the museums, they visited the local patisseries. Candace recalls, "She was laughing about it, about how funny it was that we'd visit bakeries, not museums. And as she was laughing, I found myself back there in the moment. I was smelling those scents. The vanilla, the chocolate, the aroma of fresh-baked bread. And"—she paused on the phone with me, searching for the right way to describe it—"it opened me up. The memory of the places, the food, the taste, the bonding with my mom. Not in one big flash of insight, but the more I thought about it, the more the doors opened in my mind. I went from dead-stop to opened-up in one memory."

Candace found a local cooking school, enrolled, and there, with her senses heightened, the signals became ever more specific.

"I knew, as I stood there scooping out the innards of some bird, that I didn't like cooking. It was *baking* I loved, and I loved everything about it. The fragrance and the feel of the ingredients. The fun, creative, make-people-happy side of it. I even loved the science of it. That you take these simple ingredients and five minutes later they're blended, and fifteen minutes later you actually see the cake rising. You can watch the change happening from flour and egg and butter and coloring and end up with this . . . this creation. It mesmerized me. I swear, if anyone would have offered a 'science of baking' class, I would have signed up in a heartbeat."

She started a mini catering business out of her kitchen, honing her skills, refining her craft, understanding the market. And then, when that went well, she nosed around the neighborhood looking for the right location to open a store. With San Francisco still struggling, she made the leap to Los Angeles and Sprinkles was born.

"I've missed out a lot, of course," she says. "The gut-wrenching risk of putting your life savings on the line. The worries about the move to health-conscious L.A. The seeming impossibility of persuading any landlord that a cupcake shop would be able to survive long enough to pay the rent. The missed vacations, the disappearing act from San Francisco, the unreturned phone calls to friends, the fear that it was all going to prove to be some horrible, naive mistake." Yes, Candace had to endure all of that, and yet, to hear her now, she didn't endure it so much as power through it.

"Once we got started, it seemed as though all resistance fell away. Or maybe it was just that *my* resistance fell away. I didn't know how it was all going to end up, but I knew where it was coming from. I knew where it began. And I had faith in that beginning."

Anna and Candace made their choices in the same way. They quieted their mind—Anna flipping through clippings, Candace laughing with her mother. They received the signals life sent them. They investigated the details of these signals—Anna discovering that she always flipped to the back of the *Hollywood Reporter*, Candace discovering she loved baking, not cooking. And only then did they transmit the signals out into the world in the form of actions, goals, and plans. And because both Anna and Candace built their intentions out of strong-moments, these intentions were guaranteed to be the trustworthy kind.

Moving forward, this will be how you'll make your choices in life—you'll pay attention to your emotions, you'll embrace the Lead and Supporting Roles you play, you'll search for the vivid moments that make these roles unique to you, and then you'll piece together your decisions.

WHAT TO TAKE AWAY FROM THIS CHAPTER

- **Life throws a lot of moments at you.** Some strengthen you, and some don't. Take the Strong Life test and share it with others. It can help you cut through the clamer of your life and pinpoint your strongest moments.

- **Learn to quiet your mind and receive the emotional signals life is sending you. Only then start transmitting your plans, goals, and dreams out into the world.**

- **See weakening moments for what they are, take their power seriously, and promise yourself that you will act to move them out of your life.**

- **Don't "do more to feel more."** You will wind up feeling less.

- **To pinpoint in vivid detail the strong-moments in your life after you've taken the Strong Life test, try this exercise:** Take a pad and draw a line down the middle of it. At the top on the left write a big "+" sign, and on the right mark a big "−" sign. Carry the pad around with you and anytime you find yourself in a moment where you feel successful, in flow, in control, energized, scribble it down in the "+" column. Write it right then and there, in the moment; don't wait until the end of the day or the week—you won't be specific enough. Anytime you feel the opposite—unsuccessful, you can't concentrate, out of control, panicked—scribble it down in the "−" column. After you've done this for two weeks, run down each column and pick out two strong moments from each aspect of your life. Write each strong-moment down and keep it safe (a bedside drawer, a diary, deep inside your PDA somewhere).

- **Always sweat the small stuff.** Look to the details of the moment to guide you. One way to identify these details is to look at your calendar and mark an S for strength or a W for weakness by each activity in the coming week. After each activity has happened, check back in to see whether your prediction was right. If it wasn't—if an S became a W, or vice versa—take a few moments to search for the details that made the difference.

- **To find the right career, look backward.** Read through old diaries. Sort through boxes of articles and pictures. Ask your mom what you were like as child. Visualize yourself on your elementary school playground. Start with one clear detail that you know to be true, and then slowly widen your lens.

8

ACCEPT WHAT YOU FIND

How can you honor what is true about you?

The thing that is really hard, and really amazing,
is giving up on being perfect and beginning
the work of becoming yourself.

—ANNA QUINDLEN (b.1953), American author and journalist

You search for strong-moments, not so that you can change yourself, but because these moments will guide you to make wiser choices. You search for strong-moments because, of all the elements of your life—your goals, your dreams, your relationships, even—they can be trusted the most. You search for strong-moments because in them you will find your truth.

And this truth is powerful medicine. It can free you from the confusing, overwhelming, regret-and-guilt-inducing illusion that you have thousands of possible "right" choices. You don't. Look closely and you'll see that only a very few choices actually honor your truth. These very few choices are the ones you must make. And when you make them, it will be with the confidence that you are being true to the truest part of you. Acceptance of who you are cures you of excess choice.

Good stuff, this medicine.

And yet, this truth can work its miracle only if you truly accept what you find. As you've no doubt experienced, this is far from easy to do.

What's Stopping You?

Look back over your life. Are there times when you rejected what you knew was true about yourself? Times when you heard a small voice calling you, but you turned your head away, and listened more closely to the voices of others? Times, even, when you deliberately drowned out this voice with your own shouting and claiming?

When you did it, why did you do it? Why couldn't you accept the truth about you, make your choice, and move on? Let's look at a few possible reasons.

"I'm Scared of Where This Leads"

Was it that you didn't like where this truth led you? This fear of where it all leads certainly slowed Charlie. Even after she managed to identify certain strong-moments in her life, she didn't fully embrace them because she knew they would lead to a difficult conversation with her husband, a conversation fraught with risk, a conversation she didn't know how to frame without sounding like a whiner. So she didn't have it.

Where does your truth lead you? If it leads you to give up a profession in which you've already invested thousands of dollars, or if it requires you to earn a lot less money, or to move to another part of the country, or to go back to work when your children are still very young, no wonder you shy away from it. Its consequences appear too impractical, too disruptive to your way of life. Easier to ignore it, put it off for a while, wait for a more convenient time.

"I'm Dutiful"

Or maybe the problem isn't where the truth leads you. It's other people. Other people's expectations of you can be extraordinarily persuasive. And damaging. Not that they want to damage you. It's just that they have expectations of you, and you are carried along by these expectations, until you come to believe that *their* expectations are *your* truth. You're dutiful.

The other day I was giving a presentation to a group of about two hundred graduate students at Northwestern University's Kellogg School of Management. The presentation was over, and I was peering into the darkened auditorium looking for questions. A hand in the back went up.

"What can I do about my weaknesses?" the hand asked. "I have a particular weakness that ruins everything I do. How can I manage around it?" It was a young woman's voice. I could make out her shape, sitting low in her chair, a white notepad open on her lap.

I've been asked this question many times before and have written about it in my previous books, so I slid easily into a familiar response.

"Well, first, you can just stop doing it and see if anyone cares, or even notices—before you do anything else, try this. Second, you can try to team up with someone who is strengthened by the very activity that weakens you. Third, you can keep offering your strengths and see whether the *best* of your job gradually becomes *most* of your job. Or finally, try looking at your weakness from a different perspective, a perspective that strengthens you—if you love serving clients but hate being in meetings, try to see how the meeting will result in giving better service to your clients. Meetings may never be a strength for you, but at least they won't drain you as much."

She listened politely enough, but I could tell that my answer hadn't helped her—no sitting up, no scribbling in her notepad. She wasn't disengaged or dismissive; she just needed a different answer from me. She tried again.

"What happens if your weakness is so much a part of your life that you can't stop doing it, and you can't team up with someone else to help you, and you can't find a better perspective on it? What then do you do?"

"How much a part of your life is it?" I asked, trying to get a handle on things.

"Constant," she replied. "At home. When I'm driving to school. In the classroom. It's there virtually all the time."

There's not much you can say to this, theoretically speaking, so I gave up. Jumping down from the stage, I walked slowly up the aisle toward her and asked, "Would you mind sharing with me what this actual weakness is?"

No answer.

I kept walking and was halfway up the aisle when she said, "I can't read."

"I'm sorry?" I stopped.

"I can't read. I have severe dyslexia."

Released by her admission, she told us her story in short, intense bursts. She was a graduate student. She'd just completed her second master's degree and was planning on coming back in the fall to start her doctorate. She had a great idea for her thesis, "but I just don't think I can do it. Both my parents are academics, and I know they want me to follow in their footsteps. And I want to as well. I love to do research and to study. I've fought this dyslexia my whole life. I even refused the special time dispensation they give dyslexic students for my SATs. I wasn't going to let it beat me."

A silence, all of us waiting, knowing it had.

"But I'm so tired. Every book, every newspaper, every online article. Even the street signs. Every written word drains me."

A shorter silence.

"I just don't think I can do this anymore."

You may know how she feels. You've listened more closely to other people's voices than you have to your own, and with all the best intentions in the world, you've allowed your life to become an expression of their expectations. It can work for a while, even a long while, with your sense of obligation providing you purpose and direction. But in the end, the truth of who you really are rises up and scrapes against the life you are living. And it gets so tiring to push it down, to keep it underneath, until finally your surface cracks and it breaks through: "I just can't do this anymore."

Fortunately for this woman, I could suggest one possible solution: the American Dyslexia Association provides a service that offers thousands of textbooks and articles on audio. With reading out of the equation, this woman could choose to continue her studies without the burden of the written word. Or she could choose to take her life in a different direction. But whatever her choice—and I don't know which one she made—at least now she could make her life choice based on *her* truth, not her parents'.

"I'm Ambitious"

One final reason self-acceptance can be so hard is that the truth you find flies in the face of what you've always believed about yourself. This one may be the trickiest of the lot, because both voices, the voice leading you astray and the voice telling you the truth, come from within. There are no *practical* obstacles to accepting the truth about you, and no one around you is pushing you to accept *their* truth. It's just you; you've chosen a certain identity for yourself, and the truth you've now found contradicts this identity. Shocking, distasteful, unwelcome news. So you drown it out with your ambition and your dreams and the sheer pace of your life, and you charge on and on, until, one day, seemingly out of the blue, you stop.

You may have seen this in your life or in the lives of some of your friends. I saw it in my sister's life. For as long as I can remember, Pippa (Lead Role: Creator) had wanted to be a classical ballerina. I know this is a grandiose dream and, it's fair to say, a cliché dream—how many millions of five-year-old girls put on a tutu and twirl around their bedrooms? But for my sister, it turned out to be a realistic dream. At a very early age, Pippa discovered that she could dance. Not just move in time to the music, but dance as though her spirit had always known how. She skipped off to ballet class every afternoon, and then, at thirteen, to the Royal Ballet Boarding School where years of bar work, choreography, and movement classes prepared her to graduate into the Royal Ballet Company itself and become a classical English ballet dancer.

The problem for Pippa was that a classical English ballet dancer, the dancer who could take the lead role in *Swan Lake* or *The Nutcracker*, was supposed to be a brilliant technician. For example, she was supposed to be able to do four pirouettes to the left and four to the right, and then do it again, and again. And Pippa couldn't. She could do three, no problem, three to the left and three to the right. But not four. Years of practice, huge talent, but still she couldn't do what was needed to excel in her chosen field.

Don't get me wrong, she still loved to dance, and in fact during her years in school she had discovered that she wasn't just a "dancer." She was a certain kind of dancer, a lyrical dancer, blessed with expressive arms, more graceful than she was athletic. On some level she was aware of this distinction—she never felt drawn to the classical ballet repertoire, never raved about it the way she did about modern ballet. And yet, despite this awareness, she couldn't let go of her dream. She left the Royal Ballet and moved to the German State Ballet in Munich in hopes that she would be promoted more quickly from the corps de ballet to soloist. She did well in Munich—she's a worker, after all— but, still, it always seemed a struggle, as if she were fighting against some invisible resistance.

Then, finally, the big break. She was cast as Aurora in a Christmas production of *Sleeping Beauty*, her first solo role.

I was getting ready to fly over from the U.S. to watch her when I heard the news: Pippa had become sick.

"What's wrong?"

"I'm not sure," Mom said on the phone. "She's just very tired. No energy. I'm going to take her back to London."

"Do you want me to come over?"

"No. No, it's fine. She's just very tired. And sad. You can imagine."

So mom took her back home to London and put her to bed on

the foldout couch in the living room. And Pippa, the fittest, most resilient person I've ever met, didn't get out of bed for a year. Chronic Fatigue Syndrome (CFS), they called it. As with all syndromes, it had no cause, no underlying pathology, at least none the doctors could see. It was just a cluster of physical symptoms, drugging her, dragging her down, wasting her days.

Pippa is an extreme example. As is the graduate student at Northwestern. As is Charlie. But their examples reveal a fact of life: no matter how difficult it is to accept the truth about yourself, you must choose to accept it. If you don't, your truth will force you to. It's relentless.

How can you do this? Despite the practical obstacles, the expectations of others, and the passion of your ambition, how can you choose to accept what you find?

Be Trusting

Start by trusting that you are by far the best judge of your strengths and weaknesses.

This doesn't sound right as you read it, does it? You've been raised to believe that your own self-assessments are suspect, and that if you really want to know who you are, and what you are capable of, you should look to other people. People like your parents, your teachers, your friends, or your boss. They are objective. They are the best judge of you.

Let's dismantle this notion, once and for all. Other people can certainly judge your performance better than you can, but your performance is not the same thing as your strengths and weaknesses. More specifically, your strengths are not what you are good at, and your weaknesses are not what you are bad at. Think about it for a minute. Don't you have some activities in your life at which you are extremely proficient, but which bore you to tears? Because you are driven, smart, and responsible, you are capable of doing these activities. In fact, you are so good that other people have come to rely on you to do them, perhaps they have even pigeonholed you into doing them, but you would be very happy in a world in which you would never have to do them again.

Get one or two of these activities in mind, activities at which you are competent, but that drag you down.

Now that you are thinking about them, how do you feel?

What happens if I say to you, "Tomorrow we are going to spend the whole morning learning how to do these activities better"? How do you feel now?

What happens if I tell you, "Because you are so good at these activities, we are going to sort things out so that you can spend most of your week doing nothing but these activities." How do you feel now?

You feel rotten, don't you, because these activities aren't strengths. They are weaknesses. The proper definition of a weakness is "an activity that makes you feel weak." It doesn't matter how stellar your performance is, if the activity drains you, bores you, or makes you lose your concentration, it is a weakness. The thought of learning how to do it better is singularly unexciting, while the prospect of doing a great deal more of it makes you choke with panic. It's a weakness. It weakens you.

As I told the Northwestern graduate student, there are plenty of things you can do to manage around a weakness, but no matter how well you perform it, if it drains you please don't call it a strength.

A strength is "an activity that makes you feel strong." It is an activity where the doing of it invigorates you. Before you do it, you find yourself instinctively looking forward to it. While you are doing it you don't struggle to concentrate, but instead you become so immersed that time speeds up and you lose yourself in the present moment. And after you are finished doing it, you feel authentic, connected to the best parts of who you really are.

Sure, before you launch into it you may feel a twinge of anxiety—"Will I perform as well as I know I can? Will I meet my high standards?"—but when you are done with it, you're not relieved in a "Thank goodness that's over" kind of way. Instead, there's a little thrill, a frisson of excitement, and you find yourself wondering, "When will I get to do that again?"

What this means is that *you* are the best judge of your strengths. No one knows better than you which activities you look forward to, which activities make time fly by, which activities leave you with an all-is-right-with-the-universe feeling. They may be able to judge your performance better than you, but they don't know how each specific activity makes you *feel*. You do, and, as I said earlier, these feelings are trustworthy. These feelings are true. You, of all people, can be trusted to pinpoint which activities make you feel strong.

Be Bold

Acceptance isn't resignation. If you accept what you find, this doesn't mean you have to settle for a lesser life. It doesn't mean you can't have the life you want. In fact, it means the exact opposite. When you accept what you find, you discover exactly *how* you can have the life you want.

Accepting what you find means being bold. It means taking your strengths seriously once you've identified them. It can be dramatic, life-changing action, such as Candace took when she bet everything on her baking business. But it doesn't have to be—bold isn't reckless. You can start small if you like, find one new way to contribute a strength this week, and quite soon you will see the world realign itself to accelerate and increase this contribution. Not immediately perhaps, but as your appetite pushes you to keep volunteering your strength, you'll feel the world begin to tilt gradually in your favor until you find yourself running full pelt downhill.

This is what Margret Meadows discovered. Margret (Lead Role: Teacher) began her career in the sales end of the financial services business and was quite successful at it, but when she was pregnant with her first child she decided it was time to quit. That seemed the right thing to do, especially when another baby followed quickly after. Soon, though, she became lonely, trapped in a house with two children. Margret is someone who needs to be around people, so she started looking for an opportunity to do something productive with other people.

She'd heard about a woman across town who made smocked dresses. Maybe there was something in that, she thought. Her mom had been a talented seamstress; there was no reason she shouldn't be good too. So Margret took a small step. She started taking lessons. The lady was supremely talented, if sometimes a little tough on her smocking, which, Margret was forced to confess, wasn't getting as good as she'd hoped. This was frustrating. She was practicing like crazy and diligently following the instructions of her smocking sensei, but she wasn't seeing much progress at all.

Not a disaster, she thought. *I'm just doing this because I'm lonely. But still, it's annoying. My mom was good at this. Why aren't I? Maybe I should give it up and find something else to do with my Tuesday nights.*

And then one evening, as she was sitting in traffic pondering, yet again, why she was crisscrossing Nashville to subject herself to her crotchety teacher's criticisms, she realized why she kept coming back to the sessions: it wasn't the actual act of smocking; instead it was the analytical challenge of breaking a complex task—in this case, smocking—into its component parts. *That's a strange thing to get excited about*, she thought. But the more she batted it around in her head, the more compelling it became: "I love it when I can dissect a skill down into its discrete bits, and then build it back up into the complete skill."

And then, a little aha: *Maybe I could put together a class in my house. Teach a couple of my friends how to smock.* Her mind, and the possibilities, opened up a little more: *And then we could all hang out together and I wouldn't be quite so lonely. I'd have something to look forward to.* And more: *And we'd be able to make something nice for our kids to wear. And we'd save money.*

So that's exactly what she did. She set up a class in her house to teach her friends smocking every Saturday afternoon. Another small step.

She was good at it, and she loved it. And the students—her friends—loved it too. Word soon spread and before she knew it,

Margret was being invited by fabric stores to do in-store demonstrations to increase interest and demand.

The in-store lessons went well—so well that the next thing she knew, she was being approached by a knitting magazine called *Sew Beautiful*. "We run knitting and sewing conferences," they said. "Why don't you take the stage at next month's conference in Birmingham? Instead of sitting in front of a small class of people, you can teach knitting, sewing, and quilt making to five hundred people at a time."

This seemed like a fine idea to Margret. Wouldn't it be good to be able to teach more people, to share these skills with as many as possible? So she went to Birmingham, and then to Atlanta, and then to Orlando, and pretty soon she was away most every weekend, teaching at conferences all across the South.

And then (there are a lot of "and then's" when you're living a strong life), she caught the attention of an Italian sewing machine company. They could see how effective she was at demonstrating complex tasks, making them accessible and fun, so they had an idea for her. "What if we pay you to demonstrate our product?" they asked. "It's a great machine. You can show everyone at the conferences how to use it to make stitches that appear hand-sewn."

"All right," said Margret, and she signed up as their U.S. spokesperson.

Much like Candace, when Margret took her strengths seriously, the world opened up for her. Whereas with Candace the change was immediate and dramatic, for Margret it was incremental, an evening here, a weekend there, until she wound up the national spokesperson for one of the world's largest sewing machine manufacturers.

You'll find the same. Though your strengths may limit your choices, they will, little by little, expand your world.

After a year of sickness, my sister finally relinquished her dream of becoming a classical soloist. Her long illness had given her time to think deeply about her best moments in dance, and to become increasingly specific in understanding her strengths. She sought out the best modern ballet company in the world, the Nederlands Dans Theatre, and applied for an audition. One audition became two, became five, became a visit to the company in Holland, and finally, a one-year contract. She joined the company and spent the next ten years—ten wonderful, challenging, CFS-free years—expressing her unique strengths in dance.

Today, at thirty-nine, her dance career over, she has her master's degree in fine arts and teaches modern ballet at the London School of Contemporary Dance.

Her life hasn't been one lifelong smile of happiness, nor has it been a particularly glamorous life—not with two kids, a choreographer husband, and a basement apartment in West London. But it has been a strong life, borne from her willingness to accept her truth, and to act on it, even when it led her to reject a lifelong dream.

Be Gentle

Interview any happy, successful woman and you will discover that she has faith in herself. The specifics of these women's faith vary, but all of them believe that, no matter how dire their situation, they will be given guidance as to what to do.

No, it's more specific than that. It's more accurate to say, all of them believe that the *purpose* of their situation in life is to teach them who they are and what they can offer the world. They never give up on this purpose.

You may agree with their perspective, or you may see it as a rationalization. No matter. Talk to any happy, successful woman, and you will hear it. It's not a passive perspective—as we've seen, none of the women we've met so far could be accused of being passive. It is a hopeful perspective. It is optimistic. It is, in the end, gentle.

"Gentle" in the sense that these women don't judge themselves. They don't ruminate on their lot in life, turning the events over and over in their minds, churning through all of the what-ifs and the why-me's and the what-was-I-thinking's. Instead they are—and I know this is a strange word to choose—peaceful. Regardless of their situation, they search for strong-moments, and, whatever they find, they allow the energy of these moments to enter their lives and guide them. Even if it leads to unpleasant or difficult decisions, still they let it guide them.

In this sense, they are both forgiving of themselves and demanding of themselves. They are both gentle and resolute. In fact, the more I've talked to these women, the more I've come to believe that the two are connected: they are resolute *because* they are gentle.

All of the women we've met—Anna, Candace, Margret, Pippa, and even, as you'll see at the end of the book, Charlie—share this same distinctive perspective. The writer Max Ehrmann, in his poem "Desiderata," captured it well:

> *Beyond a wholesome discipline,*
> *be gentle with yourself.*
> *You are a child of the universe,*

no less than the trees and the stars;
you have a right to be here.
And whether or not it is clear to you,
no doubt the universe is unfolding as it should.

This might appear soft or fatalistic in a poem, so, to give you a sense of what this gentle-but-resolute perspective looks like in the real world, let me close the chapter by telling you about Diane. As you'll see, when confronted with a life turned upside-down, Diane's gentle approach to her own situation led her to decisions few of us would have had the courage to make.

Between Christ and the Cross

Diane was awakened at 3:00 a.m. by a call from her husband, Brian.

"There's been a mistake. I'm down here at the police station. Can you come and pick me up?"

No, she couldn't. Their two little boys, Stephen and Max, were fast asleep, and she didn't think it wise to wake them up and drag them downtown. So she called one of their friends from church.

"Something's happened. I'm not sure what. Can you go to the police station, find out what's going on, and collect Brian? I'm here with the boys."

"Sure."

An hour later, the phone rang. It was the friend.

"Do you have Brian?" she asked.

"No, I don't."

"Why not? What's going on?"

"This is serious, Diane. The police won't release him."

"What? Why? He's a pastor!"

"They caught him running away from a young woman's apartment. She was raped. They think he did it, and that he's done this many times before."

A man had been terrorizing the city for the past year. He would break into an apartment, always a young woman's, hold her captive for two hours, sometimes more, during which he would either molest her or rape her. He'd done this at least ten times in the last twelve months.

Brian, a serial rapist? *That's crazy*, Diane thought. Crazy. He was the pastor of one of the city's largest churches! He was just finishing his doctorate in theology! He was Stephen and Max's daddy! Crazy. Surely the police had made a terrible mistake.

But they hadn't. The first week in jail Brian proclaimed his innocence. During the second week, he admitted to one rape, and by the end of the third week he confessed to all of them. In a blur of publicity and legal jargon, he was sentenced to ten concurrent life sentences, and, with stunning speed, life as Diane knew it was over.

Talking to her, I find it hard to picture her in those first few desperate weeks. Today I see a smiling, confident woman, proud of her professional accomplishments, and prouder still of her two grown boys. There's no hint of a tragedy in her past. After she tells me about it, I look for signs—anger, perhaps, or loneliness, or guilt—but there's nothing. Only a memory, a deeply sad memory, to be sure, but not one that cuts her every day. She's remarried now—*How did she ever trust anyone again*? I wonder—and they have another child, a twelve-year-old girl.

"My new husband's the real hero in all this," she tells me.

Maybe. Right now the heroine seems pretty impressive.

"What did you do in the weeks following Brian's sentencing? How did you even put one foot in front of the other?" I ask, trying to imagine how anyone in her situation could possibly make sense of the world. Where would you even start?

"I started with my faith," Diane replies. "Up to this point in my life, I was quite naive and sheltered. I had an image in my head of how our life would unfold—Brian would build his church, I would work, the kids would have a stable and loving family, and we would all worship together—but I had never looked beyond this image. Now I was forced to, and, as I looked at our new life, I knew I would have to choose: either I would reject my faith, or I would recommit myself to it tenfold. Either I was going to blame God for what happened, or I was going to ask him for help. I chose to ask him for help. And he did. He guided me."

"What did he guide you to do?" I asked.

"Well, my first thought was for the boys. When so much of your world is destroyed, all you have left is the core of who you are. At heart, I feel I'm a teacher. It's what I love to do—not every parent loves to teach their kids, but teaching the boys how to do something has always been one of my most precious moments. So I fell back on that and asked myself, 'What do the boys need to learn in a world without a father?'

"The answer I came to was that they would need positive examples of what a good man looks like. Their father had made some very bad choices, and soon enough I would have to tell them all about him. And when I did—they were nine and seven when I told them—I knew they would ask questions about how he could have made those choices, and even, whether they had some of him in them. Truly hard questions. I figured that if they had some real-life examples of what good men did for their families, they would have a counterweight to all the negative thoughts about their father. So I decided we should move in with his grandmother."

"I'm sorry. *Whose* grandmother?"

"Brian's grandmother. My ex-husband's grandmother. We moved in with her."

"Why her?"

"Because she lived far away, among the cotton farmers of northern Louisiana. These farmers were good men. They lived a simple, hard-working life. It was a small community, and I hoped that they would welcome us in and teach my boys how to be men."

"What did his grandmother say?"

"She was pleased for the company, but, sure, it was hard. On both of us. Most evenings she and I would sit at the dinner table together, and she would tell me that Brian was sick, that it wasn't really his fault—she actually wound up paying for a bunch of tests to try to prove that his brain had been damaged by an old football injury. And I would keep my peace—if I were in her shoes, I know I would have been just as protective of my grandson."

"How long did you stay there?"

"Five years. And aside from those nightly conversations, they were good years. The neighboring farmer and his wife took my boys in and spent time with them, and gave them a strong sense of family life."

"And what happened to your marriage? Did you divorce him right away?"

"Well, no. That was the other big decision I made. Everyone was telling me that I should end my marriage immediately, but I couldn't do it. I knew I would be completely justified in doing so, but I didn't want to be pressured into doing something I didn't understand.

"Even in the confused days after the sentencing, I knew myself well enough to know that I crave answers. I love to learn. Or, in this case, I *needed* to learn. I needed to be able to explain to myself what had happened. Why do men rape? What is it exactly? Is it sex or violence or power? And what part had I played in it all? Of course, I hadn't made Brian a serial rapist—I knew that was a ludicrous thought. But still, I was in the middle of the situation. When he told me he needed to go jogging late at night after working on his thesis, should I have known something was wrong? Could I have stopped it? What other clues did I miss?

"Before I divorced him, I wanted answers. So I read books dealing with rape. I interviewed rape victims. I visited him in jail many times and asked why. It gave me a focus, somewhere to direct my pain and anger."

"What did you learn?"

"Well, I learned a lot about rape, of course—that it is about power and control, not sex. And I learned that I was connected to so many other women. I'd go visit him in jail and see all these mothers and wives and sisters coming to see their men—it gave me the sense of not being that different from them, that we were all walking the same walk. It gave me comfort.

"And I learned how caring people can be to one another. You'll think I'm nuts, but while he was in prison Brian would make leather goods— belts, bags, wallets—and I would host little events where I'd sell them, kind of like a leather Tupperware party, in order to raise a little extra money. And my friends would all come around and buy them."

"Er, yes, that does sound a little weird," I admitted.

"Yes, it was, but give me a break," she laughs. "I was a little disoriented at the time. It took me a few years to realize that none of my friends ever used what they bought—I'm like, 'Mm, I've never seen her carry that bag she bought last Christmas.' Sometimes I'm a little slow," she says, still chuckling. "Even though they didn't really understand why I hadn't divorced Brian yet, they still wanted to support me. Fantastic people.

"But the most important thing this learning did was give me power. Brian had taken my power away from me. By falling back on my love of learning, I seized it back. And one day, after visiting him in the jail, I felt a calm come over me and I knew that I was ready to move him out of my life. I haven't been back since.

"I started divorce proceedings. When the court date arrived, I went down to the courthouse with my father and brother, and as I stood there looking at the docket, trying to work out which courtroom we'd be in, I saw the names of the three divorce proceedings for that day. The docket read: *Christ v. Christ*; then my name, *Garvin v. Garvin*; and last, *Cross v. Cross*.

"I called my father over to show him it was real, and said 'You know, Dad, there's nowhere I'd rather be right now than between Christ and the Cross.'"

God willing, you will never have something so awful happen to you. But no matter what setbacks you face in life, be gentle with yourself. Search for the few strong-moments in your life, rally around these few certainties, and allow them to guide you out of the valley.

WHAT TO TAKE AWAY FROM THIS CHAPTER

- **Accepting what you find frees you from the illusion of a thousand "right" choices.** Only a few choices honor the truth you've found. Stick with these.
- **Your strengths are those activities that make you feel strong.** Your weaknesses are those activities that make you feel weak.
- **Trust yourself.** You are the best judge of your strengths and your weaknesses.
- **You will discover your strengths by looking closely at the strong-moments in a regular week of your life.**
- **It can be very helpful to describe your strengths in your own words.** To capture them, try this exercise: Start with one strong-moment and choose the verb—what were you actually doing? (Tip: make sure the verb is something *you* are doing and not what someone else is doing *to* you.) Then drill down into the detail of what you were doing—does it matter who you were doing it with, when it was happening, what the purpose was? Using the verb you picked and the details you saw, write one clear Strengths Statement beginning with the phrase "I feel strong when I ..." When you are satisfied with one, write two more. These Strengths Statements, written in your own words, will keep you focused and on track when the world yanks and tugs.

- **Acceptance means take action, no matter how small.**
  Volunteer your strengths to the world, and little by
  little, the world will shift in your favor.
- **When you hit a setback, be gentle with yourself.**
  Look at your Lead and Supporting roles and use them
  as a map. Follow them and they will guide you out of
  whatever mess you are in.
- **Be open to the hardest times.** They can reveal
  precisely where you have the greatest strength.

STRIVE FOR IMBALANCE

How can you create your strongest life?

If you look at what you have in life,
you'll always have more.
If you look at what you don't have in life,
you'll never have enough.

—OPRAH WINFREY (b. 1954) talk show host, producer, philanthropist

W hen someone tells you to try to have greater balance in your life, your immediate and appropriate reaction is a spasm of disbelief. "Balance?" you ask yourself. "How does that work? For every extra hour at work find another hour at home? For every extra kid at home, reduce my workload by exactly the amount my new child requires? For every school play I should attend, cut out a presentation on the road? For everything I say yes to, say no to something else? Is that it?"

No, it's not. Of course it's not. Balance occurs when the sides of a scale are equally weighted and a perfect equilibrium is reached. As you try to balance all the different parts of your life, you discover that there's only one precise point where the scales are perfectly balanced, and at every single other point the scales are tilting one way or another. This is what your life feels like most of the time—a constant state of tipping, lurching back and forth, the contents of one part of your life sloshing and spilling over into another. You find yourself thinking about your kid's birthday party while you're at the photocopier. You're worrying about how your boss is going to react to the marketing plan—the one you promised last Friday even though you knew Friday wasn't going to work—as you drive to the movies on Saturday night. You can't stop thinking about your mother's worsening health as you drop the kids off at school; and then, when you're at work, you start worrying about why your daughter got a D on her report card for her behavior in class.

Ignore Balance

Not only is work-life balance nigh on impossible to achieve, even if you did manage to achieve a perfect state of equilibrium, it wouldn't necessarily fulfill you anyway. There's nothing inherently fulfilling about "balance." Yes, balance gives you a firm foundation, a sense of being in control in your life, and when you find it you are poised to move. And yet you are not moving. Any movement implies a tilt, a tipping, a reaching toward something. Balance is the opposite of movement. When you are balanced you are stationary, holding your breath, trying not to let any sudden twitch or jerk pull you too far one way or the other. You are at a standstill.

This precarious, motionless state is not worth striving for. It's the wrong life goal.

Strive for fullness instead. You don't have five different selves that you can keep separate. You have one life. One mind. One heart. One cup, if you will. Your challenge is not to separate one cup from another, erect boundaries between each, and then somehow balance them all. Your challenge is to move your life, tilt your life, intentionally imbalance your life toward those few specific moments that will fill your one cup.

How to Intentionally Imbalance Your Life

To begin with, in each domain of your life—such as work, family, marriage, faith, and friends—identify at least two strong-moments and write them down. In some domains, such as work or family, you may find more than two—that's okay, look carefully at your Lead and Supporting Roles, do the note-taking activity I described at the end of chapter 7, and then write down as many as you find. In some domains you may barely be able to pick out two—the "health" area, perhaps, or the "taking care of my parents" area. But keep searching anyway, because in each domain you must be able to imbalance your life toward at least two specific strong-moments.

I was interviewing someone the other day and she asked me, "If one part of my life breaks down, does it affect every other part?"

"What do you mean?" I asked.

"Well," she replied, "last year everything went haywire in two parts of my life—my relationship with my husband and my work. I felt like a failure as a wife and as a professional. I was lost. So I retreated and retreated, back to the only thing I knew for sure: I knew I wanted to be a fantastic mom to my daughter. I poured everything into being there for her, driving her to school, picking her up, taking her to dance, practicing with her. I thought if I overfilled this one part of my life, it would trickle down and fill up all the other parts."

"Did it work?" I asked.

"No. I felt great as a mom, but the strength I got from that didn't seem to make me feel any better about me as a wife or as a professional at work."

This woman discovered something that you may already have discovered: strength in one part of your life does not compensate for weakness in others. If, as happened to her, some of your responsibilities start to weaken you, you won't get your strength back by retreating to one area of responsibility and filling it to overflowing in hopes that the spillover will fill up the rest of your life.

There's simply no getting around it: *each part of your life must contain strong-moments.* Without these moments, you will feel less and less appetite for this part of your life, and so, whichever one it is—marriage, work, friends—you will find yourself doing less of it, feeling less effective at it, less in control of it. Over time, it will suck the energy out of all the good parts of your life.

So stop, take stock of each responsibility in your life, and do everything you can to find at least two strong-moments. These moments won't necessarily be of the same power in each part of your life— the moments with your kids will probably fill you up more than the moments in the gym (though maybe not; we're all different). But so what? You don't need balance. You need fullness. And each area of your life needs to do its part in filling you up.

Once you've identified these moments be *deliberate* about creating them. This can be as straightforward as putting them in your planner so that you can prioritize and look forward to them. Or you could create a routine or ritual that becomes part of the structure of your week. Or you could make a commitment to your spouse or to a friend so that they then hold you accountable for making these moments happen.

Then, *investigate* them. View each strong-moment from a new angle, or a new perspective. When you discover something novel in a strong-moment, you'll find not only that it's easier to keep paying attention to it (the research shows that, even in six month old babies, novelty attracts attention) but also that the novelty itself is its own reward. "I never noticed that before," you'll think. Or "I hadn't realized that . . . " and your discovery will delight you. (If you're looking for inspiration, return to your Lead and Supporting Roles and see whether they can offer you a new vantage point.)

And finally, whenever they happen, *celebrate* them. This doesn't necessarily mean cheering, singing, and putting on party hats. The full meaning of 'celebrate' is to hold up something so that it can be honored. So if you talk about the moment with others, you are celebrating it. If you come up with new ways to make it special, you are celebrating it. If you capture it in a photograph, a blog, or a diary, you are celebrating it. If all you do is make yourself more conscious of the moment as it happens, you are celebrating it.

On the flip side, if you can't find any strong-moments in a particular domain of your life, your choices become more limited. Initially, I'd encourage you to keep on searching for some specific strong-moments, no matter how small or insignificant they may seem at the outset. To help you, look back at your Lead and Supporting Roles and see if they reveal an aspect you may have missed.

Failing that, you must find a workable way to diminish, even cut out entirely, this part of your life. This might seem socially unacceptable, verging on the impossible—"How could I possibly stop playing with my kids? Shouldn't all mothers love playing with her kids?"— but, if you truly cannot find any aspect that strengthens you, you need to face up to this truth and deal with it. In the above example, this doesn't mean you stop hanging out with your kids. It means you confess to yourself that you are not the kind of mom who loves to get down on all fours and play endless car-racing-crash games with your three-year-old's Tonka trucks—you're no Motivator. Instead you draft your spouse or some other goofy family member to do this, while you get your mom-kicks from other sorts of moments— organizing fabulous play dates, say, or listening and soothing when your child's feeling most vulnerable.

Be deliberate about creating strong-moments, investigate them, and celebrate them, and you'll find that all sorts of good things will start to happen:

- *You'll save a lot of your time.* Activities that don't help you create these strong-moments will drop further down your list of priorities. Many will fall off completely.
- *You'll free yourself from manic perfectionism.* With your focus on creating a few specific moments in each aspect of your life, you are freed from trying in vain to do everything well.
- *You'll feel more purposeful.* You are now targeting something specific, rather than being yanked around by everyone else's demands.
- *You'll wind up being able to do more for others.* Though you

begin by focusing on what *you* need, your strong-moments will generate the strength you need to handle everyone else in your life.

- *Your life will come to feel more balanced.* It won't actually be balanced—you won't be devoting the same amount of either time or attention to each domain of your life. But it will feel more balanced because each part of your life will now be giving you energy—all-around strength.

Carolyn, a participant in the Career Intervention workshop, shows you what this can look like. When I met her, she was a twenty-nine-year-old teacher, struggling to stay enthusiastic about her role.

"I've always had a passion for teaching," she told me. "But last year, my eighth year of teaching, I started to lose my passion for it, and it kind of freaked me out. At the end of last year I couldn't wait for summer because I was so frustrated and I had to get away from teaching. I thought I would get that feeling back of wanting to be here at school, but I don't have it and it's only the first couple of weeks of the new semester. I'm scared I'm on this downhill path. These feelings are pretty new for me, and I want to know how to make them stop."

Was it that she had chosen the wrong career? Or maybe that she had just reached the end of her tether and burned out on teaching? No, neither. When I pressed her on it, I could see that she still loved teaching. Carolyn had simply neglected to pay attention to the specific moments that invigorated her and had instead filled her life with other activities—she was the head volleyball coach for her high school; she sat on the committee for the gifted and talented program for her school; she represented her district on a committee to design new linguistics programming. Each of these was done for good reason—"The linguistics programming is great experience and will enhance my résumé"—but each consumed time and drained her of energy. Energy she needed for her students, their parents, and her fiancé.

Trying to balance everyone's needs, she stayed later and later, grading tests, preparing for parent-teacher conferences, but then felt guilty that she was never at home. So she bought her fiancé two little pugs as a tangible sign of her love. Unfortunately, work pressures being what they were, she never made it home in time to walk the dogs, which made her feel guiltier still.

It would almost be funny, if it weren't so genuinely painful for her and such a loss for the rest of us. Carolyn has a quiet grace about her. She's composed and intelligent and wise, and when I met her I found myself hoping that my son and daughter's sixth-grade teacher would measure up to her. And yet here she was—the kind of teacher America urgently needs to keep in its classrooms—crying quietly as she contemplated quitting.

As part of our coaching time together, I asked her to take her calendar and put an S for strength, or a W for weakness, by each activity, each moment, in her week. This forced her to pay attention to the moments of her life and separate which strengthened her and which didn't. With her long list of S's and W's, I then asked her to do what Anna did with her clippings—sort through them one by one and see what emerged. Our hope was that it would surface the strong-moments that had been drowned out by the sheer volume of stuff going on in her week.

And it did. Here's one: she loved walking those darn pugs. Maybe it was the walking—she was always athletic. Maybe it was the time with her fiancé, with no cell phone and no papers to distract them. Whatever it was, this particular activity kept getting S's. So it became one of the moments in her week that she would fight for and celebrate.

Here's another: She learned that she was invigorated by her own reading and by her students' response to her reading. She told me that there was nothing quite like having the kids see her clutching a book on Monday, asking her which book, and then seeing them clutching the same book the following Monday, and knowing that she would be able to build a lesson around a comparison of her and their reactions to the same book.

This seems like such a small realization, but most realizations start small. Now that it had forced its way into her attention, it grew in power. The more she thought about it, the more vivid and precise it became. Amid all her confusion and questioning about whether she still wanted to teach, here was something she knew for certain, here was an authentic strong-moment drawn from her own working life. She resolved to rededicate herself to reading, to make it a more formal part of her lesson plans for each week, and to celebrate it with the kids and the parents.

And that's how it started for Carolyn. She targeted a couple of specific moments from each aspect of her life and went after them. Now, today, she is back to loving teaching again. I just got off the phone with her, and I wish you could have heard her. No crying, no sadness or resignation in her voice. Instead she regaled me with stories of the new biography class she's designed, where the kids have to pick a public figure, read a book about him or her, and make a presentation on their research. With her focus on creating a few specific moments in each aspect of her life, she's become more streamlined. She's still the head volleyball coach, but many other activities that don't lead to strong-moments have fallen far down the priority list, and a few, such as those committees, have dropped off entirely. She married her fiancé, they still have those little pugs, and they're thinking about maybe adding a stroller to their evening walks. Who knows what the addition of a baby will do to Carolyn's life, but as of now she's back on track, living a strong life, on purpose.

Your Attention Amplifies Everything

As Carolyn strove for imbalance, she made a discovery. The strong-moments in her life seemed to grow in influence the more she paid attention to them.

For example, when she thought about that moment when she got to talking with the student about her book, and she gave this moment the full power of her attention, door after door opened in her mind. She remembered the name of the book, that it was one of a series, that the kids were always talking about it, that she had read the first of the series but not the others, that she loved these conversations, that she hadn't had enough of them lately, that the kids never acted up while they were talking to her about books, that they liked it when she seemed to be doing the reading work alongside them, that there were other classes into which she could incorporate both the reading element and the "learning alongside" element. *Click, click, click,* just like Margret and her smocking, Carolyn's mental doors kept opening as her mind jumped forward and sideways, reinforcing her present and revealing her future.

You'll find this too. You'll find that your attention amplifies everything. Focus your attention on a moment, an event, an emotion, or an aspect of a person's personality, and whatever it is you're focusing on will become more detailed, and this detail will attract still more detail, and all of this detail will come to dominate your thinking.

You can see this amplification process most clearly when it comes to your strengths. Your strengths are a multiplier. Invest time and energy and training in them and you will get an exponential return. I know this runs counter to conventional wisdom. When asked, "Which is most likely to help you succeed in life: building on your strengths or fixing your weaknesses?" 57 percent of people would focus on fixing their weaknesses. (In fact, this weakness focus is even more prevalent in women between the ages of thirty-five and fifty-five. Of this group, 73 percent would bet their careers, their success, and their satisfaction on fixing their weaknesses.) But conventional wisdom is a poor guide. Your weaknesses—those activities that weaken you— are not your "areas of opportunity" or "areas for development." Your weaknesses are your areas of *least* opportunity, areas where you will develop the least, learn the least, create the least, contribute the least, volunteer the least, and be your least resilient.

Of course, occasionally you will have to address them, at which point you can either follow the advice I gave the Northwestern graduate student, or you can just suck it up and do them.

But most of your life should be targeted elsewhere, toward your strengths. Your strengths—those activities that make you feel strong—are where you will learn the most, create the most, develop the most, and see the greatest leaps in performance.

Some of this has to do with the plasticity of your adult brain—though your brain retains the ability to carve new synaptic connections throughout your life, it is far easier for it to carve these new connections where there are a lot of preexisting connections. Simply put, you learn most in those areas where you are already strong. (I wish that our schools understood this. Then we wouldn't have to suffer through yet another parent-teacher conference, drilling down into those few areas where our kids are struggling, and why are they struggling, and when, and how can we fix it. This isn't the subject for this book, but if you want to know how to deal with a teacher who is fixated on your kids' weaknesses, read chapter 12.)

Much of it, though, has to do with practice. We've all been taught that practice makes perfect, that you must dedicate thousands of hours to an activity if you want to get good at it. This is true, but not terribly helpful. The point isn't that top performance requires practice—obviously it does. The point is that you don't practice everything with the same degree of effort. You find yourself instinctively drawn to certain activities—Charlie sneaking off to Barnes & Noble to read systems integration books, Candace signing up for baking classes—while other activities you have to be dragged to like a child to the dentist. Naturally, those you are drawn to you practice more, and so you get better, and you practice more, and so you get better still, in a virtuous spiral, your appetites driving your abilities, your strengths driving your performance. (Of course, the spiral goes the other way too: no strength, no practice; no practice, no performance.)

So imbalance your life toward your strengths. Figure out how you can sharpen them with experience and training. Look for ways to volunteer them to your colleagues, your family, and your community. Learn to talk about them in terms of "Here's how I can help the team more" or "Here's where I can help the family most."

Don't tell us how good you are at them, or how much better you are than those around you—this is performance, and we'll be the judge of that, thank you very much. Instead, tell us not where you are *the* best, but rather where you are *at your best*. Share with us where we can count on you the most. Offer your strengths up as a way to get more things done. Talk to us about them in terms of the greater *contribution* you think you can make.

Pay attention to your strengths in this way, and they will bring you both happiness and success.

Deficit Attention Disorder

So long as what you are paying attention to is positive, this process, this amplification, can do nothing but serve you.

But be careful. "Your Attention Amplifies Everything" can work the other way too. If you are paying attention to the *negative* aspects of a moment, event, emotion, or a person's personality, then these aspects will acquire more detail. And the detail will attract still more detail, and pretty soon all these negative details will come to dominate your thinking.

We can give this negative twist a name: Deficit Attention Disorder (DAD—there's an acronym for you), and a great many of us seem to suffer from it. When we look at many aspects of our lives, our instinctive reaction is to pay attention to the deficits of the situation, to what's going wrong. In fact, virtually our entire approach to life improvement is based on DAD. The American Psychological Association has fifty thousand studies on depression and only four hundred on joy. Most marriage therapy is based on a detailed understanding of divorce. A doctor is an expert on disease, not health.

The new discipline of Positive Psychology has recently shifted the academic focus toward all that is right with us and our lives—What is joy? What is happiness?—but still today when you ask people, "What is the most effective way to solve a problem?" 83 percent say, "Find out what is wrong and fix it."

Why do we do this? Why do we allow ourselves to become so fixated on what is wrong with our lives?

Consider these two reasons. I'm not saying these are the only two reasons, but in all my research, these two are by far the most common.

We're Frightened

Jane and I walk into my son's first-grade classroom and we are, frankly, nervous. It's Open House at school, the night all the parents put on their best bib-and-tucker and come listen to the teachers explain their classroom philosophy and tell us how wonderful our little ones are. It shouldn't be an anxiety-inducing evening, but the kids' schoolwork is plastered all over the walls, and this is first time Jane and I will have seen Jack's work side-by-side with his classmates. We're not sure what to expect.

We walk in, and the first wall that confronts us is the art wall. Thirty pictures, stuck one next to another in a twenty-foot-high by twenty-foot-wide collage, each with some colorfully daubed scene, and each with the child's name scribbled in the bottom right-hand corner.

Sandwiched in a phalanx of equally anxious parents, we stand at attention, scanning the wall for Jack's artwork. And, as we scan, we turn to one another and say nice things about the paintings, little comments of approval, as though we're just here to appreciate the art, no skin in the game.

"Wow. Danny's a good little artist, isn't he? Look, that's clearly a mountain range. And what are those? Geese? They look a lot like geese."

"Isabel's talented too. That one's almost Hockney-esque with the swimming pool and the sun."

In the middle of all the color, I catch sight of the one black-and-white offering. It's a picture of stick figures. Large heads. No bodies. Limbs sticking directly out of their spindly necks. And there, in the bottom right-hand corner, is the name: *Jack*.

I feel an immediate urge to sidle over and quickly change the name to Mack or Jackie, or, failing that, to inch forward and stand directly in front of the picture, obscuring it from everyone's else's view. I restrain myself, nudge Jane, and point a low finger toward Jack's painting.

We stare in silence. And the feeling I have is fear. Not overwhelming, paralyzing fear, this is just a first-grade classroom after all. But it's fear nonetheless, a small twinge. Fear that Jack will notice the difference in quality and be embarrassed. Fear that the teachers will see the difference and think badly of my son. Fear, even, that the other parents will spot the picture, read the name, and then think badly of us.

You've had this fear. It's the fear that one of your weaknesses will undermine all your strengths and lead to some kind of failure. The fear that if you don't deal with the weaknesses of your employees they will hurt themselves, your customers, or even your reputation as a good manager. The fear that some part of your marriage isn't working and that if you don't confront it head-on, it could ruin everything else. The fear that somewhere along the way you made a terrible wrong turn in your life, and now, if you are not to waste your life, you must retrace your steps and make a different decision.

I lean over to Jane: "You know a private painting tutor, don't you? When can she start? Tuesday?"

I don't know what she would have said in reply—maybe Tuesday wouldn't have been good for her—because Jack's teacher, Lorne, poked his head in between ours and, smiling a genuine version of our fixed grins, whispered, "Come with me."

And he led us over to the other side of the classroom where the kids' math work was displayed. This work was also comprised of pictures—in the first few grades of school every subject is the subject "plus painting," thus math plus painting, English plus painting, American history plus painting—but now the pictures were accompanied by handwritten equations. Apparently the kids had chosen an equation, solved it, and then drawn a picture to represent what had happened in the equation—$2+2=4$ might have a picture of a boy with two apples being given two apples by his friend. *Voila*, four apples.

"See here," said Lorne. "This one's Jack's." And he pointed to a piece of paper with the equation $13-8=5$ scribbled on it.

"Notice how Jack was one of the few children who chose a number in the teens, and he was the *only* child who chose a subtraction equation. Everyone else went with addition."

I was shamefaced. My mission is to help people to identify their strengths, take them seriously, and offer them up to the world. I should have known better than to pay attention immediately to a weakness. But when fear grabs at you, your self-preserving instinct takes over and drains all the wisdom out.

It took a great teacher to remind me that, before I go booking a remedial painting class for Jack, I should sit down with him and talk about his math. Not to make him feel better. Not to "build his self-esteem," though there's nothing wrong with doing that. But instead because what I pay attention to expands. If I want his learning ability to expand, I must first pay attention to where he is currently learning the most. I need to become an expert in why he is drawn to math. Why he learns so much. Why he learns so quickly. Which aspects of math he learns fastest. Under which conditions he performs best. Does he like being timed, or does he freeze when timed? Does he think of numbers as abstract things with their own, elegant patterns and logic? Or does he like math because he craves structure and he sees numbers as a great way to impose order on the real world?

The answers to each of these questions will reveal a little more about how Jack learns and how he can learn more. And I won't know the answer to any of them unless I ask them. I won't know how to create more of what's working unless I pay close attention to what's working; and, of course, the same applies to you—in your career, your day-to-day life, and your relationships.

We Think It's the Best Way to Solve the Problem

The second cause of our Deficit Attention Disorder is that we think focusing on problems is the best way to solve them. No love in your marriage? Your instinctive reaction is to examine exactly what's causing the friction or the distance and then figure out what you can do to solve the problem. A setback at work? Do a postmortem exam (an appropriately lifeless, powerless phrase), tease out which weaknesses tripped you up, and then work to improve them. Unhappy in life? Let's take you back through your family history and lay bare the bad relationships, neuroses, and fears that are causing your sadness.

What's wrong with this approach, of course, is that it flies in the face of "Your Attention Amplifies Everything." The more attention you pay to what's wrong with your marriage, your work, your life, yourself, the more "what's wrong" expands. Even though you are paying attention to "what's wrong" for the right reason—you want to fix it—the more you investigate it, talk about it, relive it, explain it, the more detail the "what's wrong" acquires. And with the detail come weight and meaning and significance. Your marriage starts to be defined by what's wrong with it. At work you become acutely aware of the all the obstacles in your way. Your life feels like a junkyard pile of mistakes, regrets, and fears. And your personality? You find yourself being characterized by everything you're not. The weaknesses of your life *become* your life.

Simply put, the more attention you pay to a problem, the more insoluble the problem becomes.

This is how Deficit Attention Disorder looks when applied to Jack and his painting. Obviously, in the grand scheme of things, this is a trivial example—to Jack it isn't, but it is when compared to some of the major life challenges you may be facing. What it reveals, though, is how DAD can lead your life astray.

Jack is struggling with painting.

Why is he struggling? Because he can't draw figures very well.

All right, good. Problem identified. He can't draw figures very well. Solution: let's make painting an after-school activity for him and ask the teacher to pay particular attention to his figure drawing. Perhaps she can teach him some little tricks, shortcuts—the body and the head are footballs, one on top of the other, with the body-football twice as big as the head-football, that sort of thing.

Jack goes to the after-school class, listens to the tips, but still struggles. The teacher keeps showing him little tricks, keeps checking in on his progress. He improves a little, but he is quickly bored. He becomes distracted. He's told to focus on his painting. He gets frustrated. The next week he asks not to go. He complains all day. We tell him not to complain. So he goes, becomes just as bored and frustrated as he did last week, and greets us that afternoon even grumpier than he was last week. We tell him he should persevere, that he gives up on things too easily, that life isn't a bed of roses, that excellence takes work, that he'll thank us someday. But not today. Today he feels simply that he doesn't like painting and that all we talk about, when we talk about his schoolwork, is painting. Of course, this isn't strictly true, but it's how he feels. He becomes stressed and anxious, not least because, as the semester progresses, he realizes that the instruction "Now draw a picture" happens in every subject, with the possible exception of P.E. He starts to chew holes in his shirt sleeve. By the end of the semester, he's getting through one sweatshirt a week.

That's how DAD works. Think of any problem you are currently facing in your own life, and you'll realize that change follows the line of your questioning. The more you ask about what is wrong, what is causing the problem, and how you can fix it, the more your life moves *toward* what is wrong.[1]

The philosopher William James said as much when he asserted that "Why should we think on things that are lovely? Because our thinking determines our life." More recently Professor David Cooperrider has attacked our penchant for D.A.D. with his pioneering practice, Appreciative Inquiry, which is designed to create positive organizational change.

But in practical terms, what D.A.D. means for you is that you can never solve a problem on its own terms.

I'm going to repeat that. *You can never solve a problem on its own terms.*

The Power of Positive Attention

Instead, what you can do is refocus your attention, away from the root causes of the problem, and toward those parts and pieces that *are* working. You're not ignoring the problem—that's vague optimism, which doesn't serve anybody. What you're doing is weaving the few strong threads of the situation together so that they become sturdy enough to fend off any underlying frailty.

As an example for how this can work for you, let's look at your relationship with your spouse—if you don't have one, maybe you will someday, and then you're going to want to have read this.

Let's say you are having a problem with your marriage. It's not a devastating problem—you haven't fallen completely out of love with him, there's no infidelity, and no physical threat. But there's a problem of some kind—he annoys you; he doesn't understand you; he doesn't do enough for you and the family. Something.

Your knee-jerk reaction is to pinpoint the cause of the problem and then spend a lot of time talking about this cause, and what he, and you, might do to fix it so that it doesn't undermine all your good stuff. Your chain is only as strong as its weakest link, as the old saw says.

As you may have found, none of this works. You keep having the same conversation over and over, with him becoming increasingly defensive, and you becoming increasingly frustrated. He feels that you are characterizing him by everything he is not, and you feel that he isn't trying hard enough to change. On and on this spirals, the conversation repeating itself, with fear displacing conviction, distance replacing intimacy, mistrust undermining love, until one day you wake up separated.

There is a better way. And one of the country's leading experts in happy marriage, the University of Buffalo's Professor Sandra Murray can show you what it is. Surprisingly, in the happiest marriages each partner is not unfailingly and unflinchingly honest with the other. On the contrary, in the happiest marriages, each partner, when asked to rate the other on a list of positive qualities such as "caring" and "driven" and "forgiving" and "intelligent" and "focused" winds up rating his or her spouse higher than a group of close friends, higher than a sample of the spouse's extended family, and higher even than the spouse himself (or herself, whether wives were rating husbands or vice versa, the finding was the same).[2]

Murray and her colleagues have fancy terms for this—they call this perspective a "benevolent distortion" or a "positive illusion"—but what this finding means for you is that the first step to a happy marriage is always to look for the most *generous explanation* for your partner's behavior and then believe it. Thus, in your mind's eye, he's not disorganized; he's "creative." He's not thoughtless; he's "focused."

This isn't just mental gymnastics on your part. It's actually the creative force for a strong relationship. Even though your deliberately generous perspective may be a little inflated, it helps you feel more secure in your decision to commit to this person, and therefore, even in moments when you feel extremely vulnerable, your trust in the relationship trumps your need to protect yourself. Because you believe the best of him, when he does something that upsets you, you don't retreat and look for ways to get back at him, but instead you reach toward him. And so, over time, your generous perspective creates an upward spiral of love. It gives you conviction. Your conviction leads to security. Your security fosters intimacy. And your intimacy strengthens your love.

And when you do notice a specific flaw in your spouse, don't compartmentalize it. Don't put a line around it, give it a name, set if off to one side, and then try to balance it out with his positive traits, as in "Yes, I admit he is a short-tempered person, but on the positive side, he is also caring and creative and funny." Initially this might appear a sensible thing to do, but in fact, balancing out clear weaknesses with equally clear strengths won't help your relationship. You are giving his weaknesses too much attention, too much detail, too much power.

Instead, always view a weakness as a part of a strength. Thus, "Yes, he's impatient, but his impatience is part of why he is so effective at getting things done." Or "I know he's impractical, but if he were more practical then he wouldn't be quite as creative as he is. He wouldn't be quite as willing to blow up existing ways of doing things and look for better ways."

This doesn't mean that you should overlook bad behavior. It simply means that, as far as you can, you should try to see any behavior, whether good or bad, as a thread of a strength. This way no new information will be able to shatter your generous view of your spouse. Any new information can simply be woven right back into your deliberately generous perspective. From this generous perspective springs conviction; and this conviction creates security, and from security comes intimacy . . . and you're back to the positive spiral of love.

Finally, as and when problems do occur, don't analyze them, break them down, and ponder what they mean about him, and you, and your relationship. They don't mean anything. They just are. Every linking of two people's hopes and dreams and styles and choices is going to include some moments of conflict, moments when you think, *He just doesn't get me.* Yes, these moments are real—he really is too impatient, he really is disorganized, he really does have a mother who disapproves of you, he really does spend too little time helping around the house—and so it's tempting to amplify this reality with your attention.

Resist this temptation. Following the law of "Attention Amplifies Everything," the more you target your conversations toward this reality, the more vivid and weighty it becomes, until this reality starts to define your relationship. When you think about the two of you, it's the first thing you think about.

Instead, when a problem confronts you, shift your focus to what your relationship looks like when it's working. Ask yourself, "When we are at our best, what are we doing?" Picture in your mind's eye, as vividly as possible, when your last strong-moment together was. When was your last moment together that you looked forward to? When was your last moment together when time flew by? When was your last moment together that you wished could have lasted twice as long as it did? See one specific detail of this moment and then widen your lens, adding one small detail after another. And then intentionally imbalance your life toward this moment, make a plan for how and when you are going to make it happen again. And talk about it with each other. Remember it together. Celebrate it.

Your problems will not go away—problems never go away. But, whatever your relationship problems are, they will be starved of your attention, and quite soon they will pale in comparison to what you are choosing to build together.

The axiom "the chain is only as strong as its weakest link" leads you to fixate on all that's wrong. The practice at the heart of this book, catch-and-cradle, builds on a different insight: one link, made strong, can become the chain.

Jack's Statue

The latest in a long line of pictures Jack was struggling with was the Statue of Liberty. This one was particularly anxiety-inducing because it would be displayed in the corridor outside the classroom alongside everyone else's. Every evening in the weeks leading up to the day of the painting, he would find some way to let us know how worried he was. Our response ran the gamut from blithely reassuring (usually me), "Oh, don't worry, Jack; it's only a painting. Just do your best," to thoughtful and practical (usually Jane), "Jack, here look, I've found an online guide to drawing the Statue of Liberty and printed it out for you. Let's try it together," to hands-on educational "Let's go visit the Statue of Liberty when we're in New York" (both of us).

And then, suddenly Jack stopped talking about it. Not in a repressed, "I just can't deal with it" way, but in an "I'm through it. It's done. No sweat" way.

A couple of weeks later, we sat down at his parent-teacher conference and asked about the painting. As you'll see, the teacher reframed the problem by asking herself, "What strong-moments does Jack have in the classroom?" and "What does it look like when Jack learns best?" and "How can we apply what we know about Jack to this art project?" and, in so doing, rendered the problem irrelevant.

"I'm so glad you asked," said his teacher. "Jack and I had a conversation about it. He's a kid who really needs to know that there is a right answer, and what that answer is. What upsets him about art is that he thinks that the right answer is a perfect representation of whatever it is he's been told to draw—and, well, that kind of representational drawing is hard for him.

"I told him he was mistaken. That, yes, in art there is indeed a right answer, just like there is in math, but in art the right answer is 'whatever he sees.' That's the only right answer.

"The moment he understood this, he started to calm down. I asked him what he saw when he saw the Statue of Liberty and, as you guys would expect with Jack, what he saw was very ordered, structured, specific. For example, he saw the statue on a specific day, July

Fourth. And on that day, night actually, there are lots of fireworks. Rather than paint thousands of flashes and bursts, which would have been too chaotic for him, Jack decided to split the white paper up into sections, like cleanly cut pizza wedges, with the statue at the center, and each wedge a different vibrant color.

"Here, let me show it to you."

She reached up to a shelf behind her, pulled down a large folder, set it on the table, and opened it. As she flicked through the other paintings, I caught glimpses of some truly fabulous first-grade Statue of Libertys and tried to arrange my face so I didn't look inappropriately disappointed when she stopped at Jack's.

And then there it was. Fatherly pride aside, it was awesome. The whole page was filled with color, no white anywhere to be seen, with the Statue at the center (not a great likeness, I confess, but recognizable as Lady Liberty) and broad spokes of color exploding out from behind it. The whole picture was one big fireworks burst, a cubist-impressionist version of the Statue of Liberty lit up on the Fourth of July. When you looked at it you didn't think, *Oh dear. That raised arm, that torch, not so good.* You thought, *Yes. Yes. I can see what that kid saw.*

To solve the problems in your life—whether a hostile work environment, a sister-in-law who passive-aggressively criticizes your mothering technique, or a husband who doesn't help out at home—you must do the same: focus your attention on what "working" would look like, organize your life to create a few more of these "working" moments, and then celebrate them.

When you imbalance your life in this way, your problems don't disappear—Jack is not, and never will be, great at figure drawing; your you filter out the noise and narrow your search for your strongest moments.

Accept What You Find

When you pay close attention to your emotions, you will discover some things that will surprise you. Who knew that Charlie loved designing systems, but not implementing them? Well, after paying close attention to her emotions, Charlie did. But she didn't accept what she found. In fact, she denied it, masking it with her sense of obligation to her husband and her family. You must see through the mask of obligation to your true feelings, and you must accept them, wherever they lead. Only then will you be able to make choices without regret. Only then will you be able to offer up your unique contribution to the world.

Life will place enough obstacles in your way—money worries, difficult colleagues, a spouse who doesn't understand you. Don't let the biggest obstacle of all be your own self-denial. Acceptance means:

- *Be trusting.* You know better than anyone else which moments strengthen you and which don't.
- *Be bold.* Whatever you discover about yourself, follow it through to the actions your discovery demands.
- *Be gentle.* Not every choice you make will be the right one, but if you withhold your judgment and keep listening to the best of yourself, the next one might be.

Strive for Imbalance

Life may ask everything of you, but you cannot do everything.

work environment may always contain elements of hostility; your sister-in-law may always, on some level, resent you; your husband may never empty the dishwasher in the right way or at the right time. But these problems are simply overpowered and made irrelevant by the vividness, the detail and the momentum of the future you are creating. As you construct a future with more of the strong-moments you want, the original causes of your problem recede, until, from the vantage point of the strong life you're building, they are seen for what they are: real, but puny. Not worth much of your attention at all.

Cast your mind back to Anna, the Hollywood agent. This was her strategy. When her "friend" took credit for her idea and stole a job that should rightfully have been hers, she could have complained about the unfairness of it, dug deeper into its root causes, even raised the possibility of agency-wide gender discrimination. But she chose not to—not necessarily because these causes were unfounded, but because she realized that paying attention to them wouldn't get her anywhere. Instead, she intentionally imbalanced her life. She reframed the problem, asking herself the pivotal question, "What would 'working' look like?" And then she imbalanced her life toward this. She wrote memos about how this coordinator role would give the agency a competitive advantage. She described, to anyone willing to listen, recent examples of how the role could have helped this actor, or this director, or that studio. This wasn't simple persistence on her part. Nor was it just cheery hopefulness. Rather, it was a deliberate effort to help everyone at the agency see what "working" would look like.

And what happened? As you remember, a few months later she was offered the coordinator role in a different department. The direction of her change followed the focus of her attention.

WHAT TO TAKE AWAY FROM THIS CHAPTER

○ **Balance is almost impossible to attain, and unfulfilling when you do.** Ignore it.

○ **To strengthen your life:**

1. Be deliberate about creating specific strong-moments in your life—put them into your planner and stick to them.

2. Investigate your strong moments—look at them from new angles and you will always find some small detail to continually intrigue and energize you.

3. Celebrate these strong-moments—make a big deal of them, talk about them, share them with others.

○ **If you cannot find any strong-moments within a responsibility you've taken on, then diminish or relinquish this responsibility as quickly as you can.**

○ **The secret to a happy and successful life is not to put up boundaries between the different areas of your life.** Instead, it is to target specific strong-moments in each area. Once you do that, boundaries will emerge naturally.

○ **Since "Attention Amplifies Everything," you will never solve a problem on its own terms.** To solve a problem, ask yourself what "working" looks like, and then target all of your energy toward creating this. The problem will shrivel away.

PART 3

STRONG LIFE TACTICS

et's pause for a moment and take stock of what we've covered so far.

We know that in all developed countries where we have reliable data on happiness, women are becoming less satisfied with all aspects of their lives, relative to men, and that these negative feelings grow in strength as women age.

We know that this seeping unhappiness is connected to the sheer variety of choices that each woman must make, and that, since no one wants to return to a world of fewer choices, each woman, if she is to buck this trend, must learn how to become an expert at making choices that strengthen her.

We know that you play certain roles in life more consistently than others, and that your Lead and Supporting Roles can show you where your strongest moments can be found. We know that, to be at your happiest and most successful, you can follow the "catch-and-cradle" practice: search for strong-moments; accept what you find, no matter how unpalatable it may seem; and then intentionally imbalance your life toward creating and celebrating more of these strong-moments.

We also know that times of crisis, whether personal or professional, can be clarifying. They offer you the chance to sort through your own thinking about who you are and what direction you want your life to take.

All of this may well be enough for you. But, if you are like most of the women to whom I've presented these findings, you want more detail. You are an individual, with questions and issues that are utterly unique to you and your situation. You want more than a general prescription. You want specific advice.

I wish I could sit down with you and work through how the practice of catch-and-cradle applies to your life, but, obviously, I can't. So, in part 3, I've taken the questions I've been asked most often and drilled them down into detailed, tactical answers.

Not every situation will be relevant to your life, but I encourage you to read them all nonetheless. As you grow, your needs and challenges will change, and some other woman's question may yet prove to be just the advice you need to find your strongest life.

TACTICS FOR A STRONGER CAREER

To be successful, the first thing to do is
fall in love with your work.

—SISTER MARY LAURETTA, Roman Catholic nun

◎ I've Just Been Laid Off. Now What Do I Do?

◎ How Do I Find My Passion?

◎ How Do I Give a Winning Interview?

◎ Why Should I Throw Away Everything I've Invested in
My Career to Pursue My Strengths?

◎ How Do I Conquer My Fear of Change?

◎ How Do I Conquer My Ego?

◎ Am I Too Old for a Career Change?

◎ Did I Waste My Money on an MBA?

◎ Am I Wrong for Not Wanting More?

◎ Should I Focus on Becoming an Expert, or Should I Cross-Train?

◎ How Do I Know If I'm on the Right Track?

I've Just Been Laid Off. Now What Do I Do?

Obviously this is a rotten situation to find yourself in. And with money worries hanging over your head, you're probably thinking that you don't have the luxury of seeking out the right role for you because you've got bills to pay and bank balances to consider.

You're not going to be able to leap out of this mess immediately, but neither do you have to give up on your goal of finding the right job, not just any job. Here's what I'd recommend as the first few steps to move your life forward:

STABILIZE YOUR FINANCES. Before you do anything, spend an evening assessing where you stand financially. How much do you need to make in order to cover your expenses every month? What discretionary expenses can you cut? How long can you last on your savings without any new money coming in?

TAKE A PLATFORM JOB. The chances are that you need to earn some money quite soon. In which case you'll have to get a job, and yes, any job will do. This job will not be drudgery; it will be a means to an end. As Anna did with her temp jobs, take it on knowing that you are using it to give you a platform from which to build your bridge to your true career. Of course, you should take the job seriously—you should work as diligently as you can and take advantage of any specific skills or any insights that the job offers. But to avoid feeling trapped by events beyond your control, see this job as a platform, a place to stop and get a firm footing.

DO YOUR RESEARCH. Find out what skills and knowledge will be needed to excel at a new role. Do you need some kind of formal education? Or can you just transfer the experience and education you currently have? If the former, seek out and meet with an advisor from a local college that offers courses in the field. How quickly can you sign up and get started?

VOLUNTEER. Nonprofit organizations are always in need of good work performed at no cost. So as you learn more about your new field, volunteer your developing skills to a local nonprofit. Get your hands dirty. Get some practice. Get a story to tell.

PREPARE YOUR STORY. Sometime soon, you are going to have to explain yourself to a hiring manager who'll ask you, "Why do you want to enter this new line of work? What steps have you taken to ready yourself? What work have you done in this area? Whom can I talk to about this work?" Prepare your story and practice telling it to anyone who will listen.

CONNECT. With your skills developing and your story becoming increasingly compelling, it's now time to reach out and connect. Join a local association in your new line of work. Attend presentations by those already in the field, and when the presentations are over, be one of those in line, ready with a handshake, a quick personal detail, and a reason to call—be specific and don't be reluctant to ask for help. Read the success stories of people in the field you want to get into, and keep track of these names. Are any of them local? How can you get into contact with them? If you did contact them, what would you ask? Take action each week to extend your network of people you know in your new field.

PARTNER UP. Your road to a new career won't be short, nor will it be without obstacles. There will be some weeks when you make giant leaps forward, and others when it feels like your life is mired in molasses. To help you keep forward momentum, find someone in your life who can hold you accountable. A buddy. A partner. Someone to whom you can make commitments and who can ask you at the end of each week, "Did you follow through?" Your journey to a new career will be one step today and a thousand over time. This partner can help you stay the course.

How Do I Find My Passion?

Start by giving yourself a break: no one finds her true passion. She starts with an inkling, a sense of something. And she *builds* her passion by working hard, paying attention to how the different parts of the role make her feel, and by then taking the initiative to push her role gradually toward those activities that strengthen her.

LOOK BACK. To find your inkling, start by doing what Anna and Candace did: look backward. Think back to your teenage years and try to remember if there were any subjects that grabbed your attention. Ask your parents what you were like as a kid. Was there anything that you got intensely interested in, read up on, and talked about incessantly at the dinner table? Don't try to have this conversation on the fly with your parents; you won't get enough detail. Instead, set aside a good thirty minutes and walk them back through time, back to when the demands and expectations of the world had yet to blanket your sense of who you really were.

PAY ATTENTION TO A REGULAR WEEK OF LIFE. If you get nothing from the past, then take your memo pad around with you for a week or two and keep track of which articles you read, which stories you are intrigued by in which magazines, which moments you found yourself looking forward to, which moments flew by, which moments made you feel like, "When can I do that again?"

BE PRECISE. No clear number one interest? Then pick one of your top three areas of interest, and start there. Do your research, narrow your focus to a role or job title, and then, as Anna did, seek out the first rung on the ladder. Then work really hard. Put in all the hours God gave, see which parts of the job excite you, if any, and deliberately push your role toward these specific parts. Always keep your attention trained on the specifics of which actual activities give you the biggest kick. These precise activities are your raw material for building your passion. Passion is useless without precision.

Always remember, passion can't be found way up in the sky, in far-flung dreams and hopes. Passion lives at ground level, in the day-to-day tasks you are being paid to do today, tomorrow, and the day after.

One last possibility you might consider is that you don't have one clear passion. You may be a Pioneer, the kind who's intrigued by many different subjects, and who pursues each of them with equal passion. If so, don't beat yourself up about it. Instead claim it, own it, and then figure out how to channel it productively. How can it make you more valuable at work? How can you use your insatiable curiosity to serve your family? What community work can you volunteer for? Make it useful.

If you don't, you may turn into a dilettante, someone who flits from one subject to another, an amateur at each, contributing nothing.

How Do I Give a Winning Interview?

Most people are nervous about interviews because they think that they are setting themselves up to be evaluated by another person. To begin with, try a shift in your perspective: the person interviewing you wants to like you. It sounds odd but more than likely, it's true. She's desperate to find the right person to fill the role and has a lot riding on making the best decision.

So present your true self. Own who you are and claim your strengths. That's all you can do, and, if you're the right fit for the job, you'll have a good shot at getting it. And if you don't, know that there is another organization out there where you will fit even better and that may well prove to be much more fulfilling.

1. How do I ensure I get an interview?

HIGHLIGHT MEASURABLE STRENGTHS. Highlight the specific strengths you are bringing to the organization and then link these strengths to measurable achievements, with the emphasis on the word *measurable*. You didn't "increase sales"; you "beat quota by 16 percent three years in a row." You didn't "give good client service." You "retained 96 percent of your clients each year." Scores are persuasive. Refer to them often.

LEVERAGE YOUR NETWORK. Many organizations value the recommendations of their current employees. If you have any inside connections, ask them to forward your résumé to the hiring manager with a recommendation. Be sure to ask your connection about the recruiting process and any tips they have for you.

2. What questions am I going to be asked?

- **What are your strengths?** Before you answer this question, share your definition of a strength as an area of your job where you are at your best, not necessarily that you are claiming to be the best—no one likes a braggart. Then follow this up with specific stories to demonstrate those strengths.

- **What are your weaknesses?** Many people try to answer this question in a way that presents a weakness as a strength. "I just work too hard, I guess!" "I'm too desperate to get it right every time." "I'm a perfectionist." But everyone knows this trick. Instead, explain that there are certain activities where you are not at your best, that you consider these activities your weaknesses, and then share strategies you've used in the past to manage around these weaknesses so that they don't get in the way.

- **Why should I hire you for this position?** Be specific. Say, "Here are the ways that I can contribute my strengths to the success/performance of this organization." Give the interviewer some real and recent examples of significant successes that you've made in other roles and how you used your strengths to achieve them.

3. What should I ask in an interview?

Serious applicants are always prepared with questions for the interviewer. Your questions should be as memorable as your answers, so take the time to get clear on what you really want to know about the role.

Here are three questions you should always ask:

- What are the three top priorities for the person in this position in the next ninety days?
- What are the key strengths you're looking for in the person you select for this position? How do these strengths relate to what this position is responsible for?
- How would you describe the company culture? Would you give me some examples of this culture in action?

4. What are the biggest no-no's in an interview?

BEING LATE. It should be obvious, but showing up late for an interview is a blatant sign that you are not serious about the role.

LYING ABOUT YOUR EXPERIENCE. Lying about your experience will haunt you. Never make up answers or tell a story about experiences that are not true. It might be tempting to embellish a little, but resist. Either the interviewer will tell you're faking it, or they will call up your references and learn that you're faking it, or worse, they won't discover that you're faking it, you'll get the job, and it'll all come out after you're hired. And you'll be fired. Much better to tell the truth and then let the chips fall where they may.

CLAIMING TOO MUCH CREDIT. Many people tell true stories about experiences but neglect to include that there were other people involved in the success. It makes sense to focus on what you did well and how you helped the team, but always give credit where credit is due. Not only do you want to be absolutely sure that your references corroborate any claims you're making, but more importantly, you'll come across as someone who makes those around her better.

BEING RUDE. It may seem obvious, but be polite to everyone you meet while waiting for the interview—particularly the receptionist. This person could be a future coworker, and many hiring managers will check in with the receptionist about their first impression of you—receptionists are masters at first impressions. You don't have to overdo it, but do be cordial and kind.

WEARING THE WRONG CLOTHES. Know the dress code of the organization and match it—try not to overdress or underdress, but if you're going to do one or the other, overdress.

5. Is there anything I can do after the interview to increase my chances of getting an offer?

DO YOUR RESEARCH. Learn as much as you can about the company: its mission, vision, values, key contributors. Get yourself ready for the second interview.

ALERT YOUR REFERENCES. Make certain that your references are aware that they may be contacted and make sure they are available to respond to a call in a timely manner. Double-check their contact information.

THANK THE INTERVIEWER. Always send a handwritten note following an interview thanking the interviewer for their time and ensuring they have the appropriate number to contact you. If you want the role (following the interview, you may not!) be sure to reinforce how you feel you can apply your strengths to improving the performance of the organization.

Why Should I Put My Current Career at Risk in Order to Pursue My Strengths?

I heard this story the other day: "A woman is swimming across a lake. She's holding a rock. As she swims, she tires. The rock is pulling her down. People on the shore urge her to drop the rock. She swims on, tiring as she swims. The people shout louder. She can barely keep her head above the water. 'Why won't you drop it?' they shout. As she sinks beneath the surface, she cries out one last time, 'Because it's mine!'"

You don't necessarily need to throw away everything you've invested in your career in order to pursue your strengths. But neither should you cling to a life you have built for yourself, when it is killing you anyway.

GIVE YOUR JOB ONE LAST CHANCE. Ask yourself first whether the job you're currently in may be right for you after all. Remember Carolyn, the teacher who had lost touch with what she loved about teaching? She felt utterly depleted by her role. She was scared that she would have to quit teaching completely. And yet, after she shifted her perspective, she rediscovered the joy of the job and is now invigorated and renewed. Your solution might be much closer to home than you think. So why not do the "S" and "W" exercise? Focus in on your strengths and, at the end of each week, pick two that create in you strongly positive emotions. Search your emotions and replay what happened in your mind. Relive those two moments. Feel again what you loved about the job in the first place.

IMAGINE THE FUTURE. An inability to imagine a future in a role is the surest sign that you're in the wrong role. So if you've looked hard at your strengths, relived those strong moments, and still you cannot get excited by a future filled with more of these moments—well, then, it's time to act. Make the decision in your mind, and plan your exit strategy. You shouldn't dance around it or second-guess it. You have to accept that your job does not and will not ever call upon the best of you and that nothing—not the money or the benefits or the time and training invested—can compensate for this. Nothing.

BUILD A BRIDGE. Chances are, you can't quit your job immediately and strike out in your bold, new direction. You probably need the money. You probably need to hang on to the benefits and secure the references. But you have to start yourself moving in the right direction. What must you do to build a bridge from your old career to your new life? What qualifications do you need? What contacts can help you? What courses can you sign up for? Commit to taking at least one action each week to move toward the life you want.

GET SPECIFIC. In job interviews, the interviewer is frightened that she will make the wrong decision and hire someone without the proven qualifications. It's her safety net against a bad hire. So if you don't yet have the right experience on your résumé, compensate by being incredibly specific about what your strengths are and why they are drawing you toward this new line of work. Write a cover letter that uses phrases like "I am at my best when . . ." and then describe a very specific activity that strengthens you. And if you want to be convincing, share the belief you have in your heart. Write down why you know—not think, *know*—that this strength will enable you to succeed in this new role. And, if you get the interview, have two or three examples of this strength in action. Practice saying the examples out loud to a friend or a spouse. Specificity gives people certainty, and certainty calms fears.

START THE JOURNEY TODAY.

How Do I Conquer My Fear of Change?

Human beings fear the unknown. Not that this is anything to beat yourself up about. Fear of the unknown is actually an adaptive trait—those of our forebears who lacked this fear, who were in the habit of wandering into dark caves with a "Ooh, I wonder what animal lives in here?" often didn't live long enough to pass on their genes. So to be cautious is actually rather sensible. Particularly when your children's well-being is involved.

Having said this, fear of "what might happen if . . ." must never stop you from seeking work that fulfills you. As I described earlier in the book, any responsibility you take on must contain within it specific moments that strengthen you. If you have chosen to work, and if your work doesn't contain any strong-moments, you are not going to be able to compensate for this lack by overfilling the other parts of your life. Quite soon, the emptiness in your working life will deplete you, and your children, young though they are, will sense it. So, if you feel your satisfaction at work draining away, and you can see another role that thrills you, don't let your concern for your family stop you from acting. Procrastination is a poor strategy when what you're fighting is decay.

So what to do? Fear is a resilient foe, but here are two ways you can beat it:

GET EXCITED. Concentrate on how excited you are about the new role. Visualize the moments in the new role that energize you. Picture yourself living these moments, achieving these victories, and feeling these thrills. Give these feelings the full power of your focus, and, in comparison, your fear will begin to lose much of its power. Remember that your attention amplifies everything.

GET SPECIFIC. Specificity is the antidote to anxiety. Ask yourself, "What does success look like in this new role? What metrics will I use to measure this success? Which particular strengths will I have to call upon in order to secure this success? What are the specific actions I will have to take right away?" Each answer will fill in the blanks of this new, unknown role, and with each new detail, your fear will dwindle still further until all that's left is a healthy prick of impatience to get started.

How Do I Conquer My Ego?

First off, know that there's nothing wrong with having an ego. Ego gets a bad rap because when we say the word we think of the words *egomaniac* or *egocentric*, but those words mean an *excess* of ego. Ego itself, the need to claim to be someone of worth, is the source of much that is noble in the world. Joan of Arc had an ego, as did John F. Kennedy, Mother Teresa, Margaret Thatcher, and Mahatma Gandhi. All believed themselves to be people who would make a significant difference. Nothing great and glorious happens without someone to claim it.

The question, of course, is to what do you connect your ego? You may choose to tie your ego to your title or your salary, and who am I to tell you to do otherwise? Many of us get a little ego thrill from seemingly silly things, such as what's on our business card or on the labels of our clothes. But, if you do this, know that that these little ego crutches lose their power if the actual activities of your work drains you. Your ego demands that you make bold claims, look for better ways of doing things, crave and see a better future. You will do none of these things if you're in a role that doesn't strengthen you.

So, if you're worried about your ego, give it its due and choose to connect it to your strengths. Your strengths are the very best of who you are, the most precious part of you. Look deep inside you and you will see that what your ego is asking of you is to honor this precious part of you. It is asking you to break free of the velvet handcuffs, and show the world all you are capable of.

You'll do well to listen to it.

Am I Too Old for a Career Change?

I know it can be discouraging to be disqualified from a role because you don't have the required degree, or because you are twenty years older than the next applicant—you will find hundreds of posts from fifty-plus women on Oprah.com's message boards, women who share your experience and frustration, and who offer stories of success and encouragement.

But know that there are steps you can take to battle these odds. Here are three you may want to try:

HIGHLIGHT YOUR ADVANTAGES. Instead of focusing on what you don't have, pay attention to what you do have. Twenty-five to thirty years of experience are gold for many employers. You have wisdom, experience, and strengths that younger applicants can only dream of, no matter how many degrees they have hanging on their walls. Practice framing your experience as an advantage. Get used to talking about how your experience has helped you, and what lessons you have drawn from it.

TAKE COURSES, ANY COURSES. This may sound odd, but it doesn't really matter what the courses are; sign up for some and take them. What many employers are worried about with older job applicants is that they will be hiring someone who is out of touch with current thinking and practice. To combat this, prove to them that you are still hungry to learn. Be ready with two or three examples of the courses that you took recently, why you chose them, what you learned, and how it will prove useful on the job.

REMOVE DISQUALIFIERS. Not knowing how to use a PDA is a disqualifier. Not knowing how to use Word, Excel, or PowerPoint or how to upload pictures onto your computer, these are all disqualifiers. You are fighting the perception that you are out of step with the modern business world. Be prepared to prove that you aren't.

Did I Waste My Money on an MBA?

No, of course you didn't waste your money.

First, it's a significant accomplishment to get an MBA. As you discovered, it takes discipline, focus, and sacrifice. And you did it. You proved to yourself that you could take a vague desire to get better and transform it into two years of diligent, brain-stretching effort. For a moment, stop looking ahead, and celebrate this achievement. There can be no excellence without celebration. This applies to everything in life—work, kids, relationships—and it sure as blazes applies to your success in finishing your MBA. You excelled. Celebrate it.

Second, you just spent two years learning the language of business. I don't know if you loved analyzing all those Excel spreadsheets, messing around with net present values, and solving return-on-invested-capital equations, but the fact that you finished the degree shows me—and anyone else—that you are comfortable "talking business." This fluency might not have netted you your perfect job right away, but it will serve you well for as long as you work in the corporate world.

And last, this MBA of yours is a lifelong calling card, something that will always serve to separate you from the larger crowd. I'm not saying that the only way to succeed in business is to get an MBA. Nor am I suggesting that what you learn in a business school can substitute for real-life experience and responsibility. But if you want something to differentiate you from the throngs of employees with similar backgrounds to yours, an MBA will serve this purpose very well.

So you didn't immediately land the shiny new job right out of business school. So what? Finding success in your career rarely happens overnight. As you've seen throughout the book, career success is a lifelong *practice*—a potent combination of paying attention, working hard, and gradually pushing your life toward the moments and activities that strengthen you. What you've got with your MBA is a one-time *advantage*. Celebrate this advantage, use it where you can, but know that you will build your career around the lifelong practice of catching and cradling your strongest moments.

Am I Wrong for Not Wanting More?

This question reminds me of how I started the book, because it all depends what you mean by the word *more*.

Do you mean more money? More responsibility? Or perhaps you're after more recognition, more status at work? Because if you truly want more of these things, turning down a promotion that brings these things with it, while not necessarily wrong, is certainly confused.

However, you may not necessarily want any of these things. More money won't bring you happiness. More responsibility will inevitably bring with it more time at work, which will mean less time with the kids. More recognition and status are lovely on their face, but, as you probably know, they bring with them greater expectations which will, in turn, pull you away from your kids.

So, from my vantage point, if you don't really want these things, it isn't wrong of you to reject a promotion that would bring them.

But what does my opinion matter? It's your life. If what you mean by "more" is that you want *more* time with your kids, *more* moments of delight as you see them figure something out for the first time, or hear them use a brand-new word, all that's important is that you confess this to yourself, get comfortable with the implications, and then orient your life toward making more of these moments happen. This is a fine and wise decision, because it springs from a desire to create more of a certain sort of moment. A sort of moment that you know energizes you.

At the beginning of *Annie Hall*, Woody Allen tells a joke: "Two elderly women are at a Catskill Mountain resort, and one of 'em says,

'Boy, the food at this place is really terrible.' The other one says, 'Yeah, I know; and such small portions.'"

The only bad decision would be to continue to strive for *more* of something that you don't really love in the first place.

Should I Focus on Becoming an Expert, or Should I Cross-Train?

If your manager is telling you to cross-train, don't fight it. Do as she suggests and try to gain as much experience as you can about all aspects of the business. Not only will this give you a more holistic view of the business, but, who knows, perhaps you will discover latent strengths you didn't know you had.

However, I wouldn't look at cross-training as the secret to long-term career success. The danger is twofold. First, that in jumping from one department to the next, you never become an expert in anything. Instead you are a permanent beginner, always learning the ropes, always asking the novice questions. Some may tell you that a fresh pair of eyes is a valuable perspective, and that all of us should strive to assume a beginner's frame of mind. My view is that this is nice in concept but impractical in the real world. In the real world, people don't want to entrust things to amateurs. They want to rely on professionals.

Which leads to the second danger: that, as the new kid in the department, you are most vulnerable when, and if, the organization has to reduce its head count. You might think that organizations would value most highly those employees who are versatile enough to slide into many different roles. But the real world doesn't work that way. If you are the least senior and have the least expertise in the department, you are the *most* likely to be cut.

The best strategy for sustained career success is to develop at least one area of deep expertise. Not only will this expertise make you more valuable to the organization, but it should also allow you to look more clearly into the future. Conventional wisdom suggests the opposite—that if you focus too tightly on one area, you will become less open to change and to new ideas. This isn't true. By deepening your expertise in one area, you become more conscious of the underlying components of your work, and therefore, as your mastery increases, you become more able and willing to play around with these components in search of a more effective way of doing things. You also become better read, you attend more professional conferences, and therefore are more likely to be exposed to new ideas and innovations. In short, your mastery makes you more creative.

All in all, mastery is your best bet for career longevity. You'll be seen as more reliable, more innovative, and ultimately more valuable.

How Do I Know If I'm on the Right Track?

I'm a great believer in your own inner wisdom, so my first answer is simply: You'll know. Deep inside, you'll know.

But if you're more of a checklist person, here are ten signs to watch out for. You'll know you're on the right track if:

- You surprise yourself by actually looking forward to going to work.
- You make detailed plans about how to do things better.
- You read books and magazines related to your work.
- You learn new skills quickly, as if you've done them before.
- You like socializing with your colleagues after work.
- You find yourself telling your nonwork friends stories about what happened at work.
- You trust your boss.
- You're invigorated, even at the end of a day of hard work.
- You feel a sense of contributing to something greater than yourself.
- You build back quickly from small setbacks.

TACTICS FOR STRONGER RELATIONSHIPS

One of the oldest human needs is having someone wonder where you are when you don't come home at night.

—MARGARET MEAD (1901–1978), American anthropologist

◉ **You Deplete Me!**

◉ **How Do I Deepen My Relationships?**

◉ **How Do I Strengthen My Marriage?**

◉ **How Do I Resolve Our Differences?**

◉ **How Do I Persuade My Partner to Support Me in a Career Change?**

◉ **How Do We Divide and Conquer?**

You Deplete Me!

I can relate. I used to work with this guy who drove me nuts. He was the sort of person who, no matter what I'd done, would have a story of how he'd done the same thing, only better. Let's call him One-upmanship Guy. You know the type: I spoke about a successful deal with a client; he countered with how his deal was more impressive. I'd come up with a great idea; he'd share how he'd already thought of that and evolved it to another level. I said I'd climbed Mount Everest; he'd landed on the moon. I wanted to like him. Really, I did. But no matter what, this guy would firmly plant himself right under my skin.

When I knew that I was meeting with him, I would try to prepare myself to walk in strong and generous of spirit, yet soon I'd notice my shoulders begin to sag as I heard him launch into yet another of his tall tales. I would look at him and I would think (never say, just think): *You deplete me.*

So what did I do? I used the STOP strategy. I'd recommend you try it too:

S: Very simply, *stop* being around him. A legitimate strategy to use for a bad relationship is to simply get out of it altogether. I know it's not always possible to avoid a person completely, but there is probably something that you can do to cut down on the amount of time you spend with this person. I kept all the important meetings that I had with One-upmanship Guy, but I pardoned myself from the lunches, the meeting sidebars, the unnecessary chitchat.

T: *Team up* with someone who sees the person differently, someone who can soften his rough edges. With One-upmanship Guy, another person on our team was really inquisitive. While I would find myself start bristling when One-upmanship Guy would start in on how he'd accomplished x, y, and z, she would be intrigued: "Tell me more about that. What else did you do?" Initially, I was frustrated. *Please*, I thought to myself. *Please don't get him started*. But little by little, her innate inquisitiveness sucked me in. I started listening to his answers, and sometimes I would hear him say something that was rather, well, brilliant. See if you can find a third person whose personality somehow oils the friction.

O: *Offer* up one of your strengths to pull him into a place where he ceases to bug you quite so much. I'm a conceptual person. I love ideas. So, with One-upmanship Guy, I made a little competition for myself. In every meeting I would bring in as many ideas, thoughts, actions, and initiatives as I could and throw them out there to see if he could really one-up me on everything. In a weird way, he motivated me to keep offering up my ideation strength, my innovation strength, my conceptual strength. And frankly, he came up with some pretty good ways to maximize my ideas.

P: Try shifting your *perspective* on the person who weakens you. Look at him through the lens of his strengths. You can always choose to characterize a person for what he doesn't bring. In my case, perhaps the problem was not One-upmanship Guy's problem; it was *my* problem. Perhaps, instead of seeing him as being in competition with me, I could have looked at his behavior as a sign of his never being satisfied. Perhaps he was one of those people who was always looking for creative ways of solving old issues, devising better ways of approaching our work, a Pioneer. I tried looking at him in this new light and, frankly, it worked like a charm for many years. What began as my problem—he weakened me—transformed when I changed my perspective. Suddenly, I had a powerful new weapon on my team.

I am not saying the STOP strategy is always going to work, but experiment with these strategies before giving up on the other person. You may find that there is a whole new relationship waiting to be discovered.

How Do I Deepen My Relationships?

There are straightforward ways you can save time in managing your relationships—for example, rather than try to return each social obligation individually, you can get them all together at a group dinner or for drinks; or, when you want some one-on-one time with one of your friends, suggest coffee rather than lunch. But I don't think that's your question. You want to know how to establish *genuine* relationships with your friends, despite how busy and distracting your life is.

Obviously each relationship of yours will be unique, but here are four practices that will help you deepen your connection to your friends:

BE PRESENT. Whether you are having coffee, lunch, dinner, or a cell phone conversation in the car, listen. You will be able to tell if you are doing a good job of listening if your friend keeps talking—the other person's behavior, not your own understanding, is the sign of a great listener. If you can't be fully present when someone is speaking, either ask to speak at a different time when you can be present, or figure out a strategy for managing yourself so that you are.

BE CURIOUS. Inquisitiveness is the antidote to assumption. It opens you to another's experience and develops your compassion. If you want closer and more meaningful relationships, be genuinely curious about the other person. Pay attention to the details of the people in your life. What do they value? What do they care about? What important things are they dealing with?

BE TRUSTWORTHY. There's no faster or more genuine way to strengthen a relationship than to keep a friend's confidences. When a friend shares a secret, they are taking a risk with you. You now have the chance to prove that you are a safe haven for them. A genuine friendship is a place where you don't have to watch your back. So find ways to show that you've got their back.

FIGURE OUT WHAT KIND OF A FRIEND YOU ARE. You aren't one kind of friend to your entire circle of relationships. Yes, your personality and your values remain consistent across people, but a relationship is an interaction, and the way your personality and values interact with each person will vary. To one friend you will be a champion and chief supporter. To another friend you will be a shoulder to cry on. To another you'll play the fool, while to another you may be the voice of reason. It may take a little while to work out what each friend draws from you, but it's worth taking the time to figure it out. Once you know what each friend expects from you, you can concentrate on meeting these expectations as best you can. This will make you a more predictable friend, and predictability engenders trust.

How Do I Strengthen My Marriage?

There will always be some elements of your relationship that are inexpressible. Well, they may be expressible, but they aren't entirely explainable. Jane and I have been married for thirteen years, and to this day there is something about her I find intriguingly mysterious. I sort of know what it is—some combination of her toughness, her compassion, and her self-deprecating humor. But that doesn't come close to capturing it, and besides, even if it did, I still wouldn't be able to explain why it appears new and exciting to me every time I see it.

You'll find lovely mysteries in your relationship. Best not to ask too many questions about them. Just appreciate them and thank God you were blessed with the eyes to see them.

Of course, this doesn't mean you can't do anything to strengthen your relationship. As I described earlier in the book, the strongest marriages are based on the practice of generosity. Both partners deliberately look for the most generous explanation for the other's behavior. This is almost impossible to do if you lack for lovely mysteries; all positive illusions—for that's what a strong marriage is—are built on genuine belief.

But if you do have something genuine at the core of your relationship, there is plenty you can do to bring this core to the surface. Not all will fit with your style, so choose the ones that do and make them a deliberate practice.

KEEP AN APPRECIATION JOURNAL. Write about the best aspects of your husband. Revisit them often. As the research reveals, your perceptions of him not only color your current reality, but they also give you confidence in your choice, they cause you to reach toward him rather than away from him, and therefore they actually create your future reality. So, when looking at him, choose your perceptions with great care. They fuel your desire.

CATCH HIM DOING THINGS RIGHT. Look for evidence that he is loving, supportive, and compassionate. He may not always show you these qualities in exactly the way you would like, but if you look for them you will find them.

FIND OUT HOW HE LIKES TO BE SHOWN LOVE. The oft-quoted axiom to "treat others as you would treat yourself" means that we should be as gentle and as forgiving of others as we hope they would be to us. It does *not* mean that everyone likes to be treated the way you like to be treated. So don't assume that your spouse likes to be shown love the way you do. There are some wonderful books on the subject of the many ways to show love to another person—*The Five Love Languages* by Gary Chapman is one of the best[1]—but no book will ever capture the uniqueness of your husband, and so nothing will substitute for your paying attention. Over the course of your marriage, watch, listen, and ask, and you will gradually build up a picture of how he comes to know you love him.

DISCOVER THE ACTIVITIES THAT STRENGTHEN HIM THE MOST. What are the strong-moments in *his* life? You may know, broadly, what his goals and dreams are—"He's a family man," "He's very ambitious," "Being of service gives him purpose in life"—but do you know when the last moment was with the two of you that he actively looked forward to? Do you know when he's in his zone at work? Do you know what exactly he wants to get out of his friendships? If you were looking at the activities in his calendar for next week, could you put S's and W's accurately by each one?

MAKE TIME TO APPRECIATE ONE ANOTHER. Amid the crazy busyness of your life, it can be hard to find the right time, or the right tone, so be deliberate about it. If you are an informal couple, simply make a point to tell him one thing every day that you appreciate about him. If you are more formal, make an evening of it. Set the stage, and then spend focused time together giving each other loving reinforcement. Tell each other all the ways that the other person makes your life better; what you notice about him that you love; how he impacts the lives of your children, if you have them. Use specific examples to illustrate what you are saying. So many of the most important things in life are left unsaid. Don't let your gratitude for the essence of him be one of them.

Of course, none of these actions is yours to take alone. Ideally, your husband will be doing the same for you. I suppose each of you could wait for the other to start, but you might be waiting rather a long time. Better for you to begin, show him what it looks and feels like to be on the receiving end of your positive illusions. And he'll be more likely to follow your lead.

How Do I Resolve Our Differences?

Disagreements, conflict, arguing: these are not typically things anyone looks forward to, but when the end goal is to find a solution that meets both your needs, conflict can actually deepen your connection. Here's a simple structure to follow:

DEFINE THE ISSUE BEHIND THE DISAGREEMENT. An issue is never a person; it is always a topic, a subject, a behavior, or an event about which there is a disagreement. Keep your language neutral. "The issue is our son's sleeping habits."

LOOK AT THE ISSUE FROM THE SAME SIDE OF THE TABLE. I mean that literally. Physically sitting on the same side of the table helps build rapport, connection, and ultimately ensures a better understanding of the other person's perspective.

ASK "WHAT WOULD 'WORKING' LOOK LIKE?" and then drill down into the detail of this with even more specific questions. Remember, your questions are generative—change follows the direction of your questions. If you ask a lot of questions about why your son is waking up at night, and what is stopping him from staying asleep, and what each of you is doing wrong when you put him down or coax him back to sleep, his sleeping problems will get worse—as will your relationship.

In contrast, if you ask what happened the last night he slept well, what happened before he went down, what he ate, how long you played with him, read to him, how warm the room was, deeper and deeper into the detail of what "working" looks like, you're much more likely to discover the solution; and the discussion might actually be quite enjoyable! Sounds unlikely, I know, but try it.

FIND YOUR COMMON INTERESTS IN SOLVING THE PROBLEM. An interest is usually related to the core of a person's well-being, so it is vital that you explore these, generously, together. Ask him straight up: "Why is this so important to you?" Once you hear from him what his interests are in resolving this issue, you'll more than likely be able to find points where your interests connect.

COMMIT TO DESIGNING A SOLUTION TOGETHER. Ask him, "What options would satisfy what is important to both of us?" Be open to the solution being something completely different from either of your original positions.

MAKE A PHYSICAL COMMITMENT. Once you've agreed to a plan of action, make a physical sign of your commitment: sign a paper or step over a line on the floor together. Shake hands, if that's all you can muster. Symbolic though this is, expressing your commitment physically makes it harder for you both to break it.

How Do I Persuade My Partner to Support Me in a Career Change?

You may be scared of trying to persuade him because you assume that his reaction is going to be negative. This is a weak place from which to begin. Do what you can to change your mind-set. Envision what a positive outcome would look like. See, in your mind's eye, your spouse agreeing with you and supporting you. By itself, your belief won't make it happen, but it will give you a strong starting point.

SET THE STAGE. Decide where and when you will talk to him about it. Pick a place in which you feel strong and centered. And then decide, in your own mind, whether you are making a presentation for why the change *must* happen, or whether you are debating whether change *should* happen. If you think you are going to have a debate, refer to the previous question. If you think you are making a presentation, try this:

PRACTICE. Whatever you plan to say, make sure to practice. Practice saying it out loud with a friend or a parent. Practice your examples, your logic, the questions you are going to ask him, your answers to his questions. Practice all of it.

DESCRIBE THE BURNING PLATFORM. First, explain why you feel compelled to make a change. Talk about the specific activities on the job that drain you, how you struggle to concentrate, how it's getting to the point where you don't want to get up in the morning. And then, talk equally vividly about the specific activities of the new job that you are drawn to. Don't start with pay and benefits and long-term career advancement—even if these are real, none of them will compensate for a role whose activities weaken you. Instead, put yourself in the middle of the experience. Own your own emotions. Make yourself— your emotions, your needs, the need to express the best of you—the burning platform.

DESCRIBE THE BENEFITS. Describe how this change will help him and the family. Obviously, don't stretch the truth—you don't want to over-reach and have your argument undermined. Just state as clearly as you can why the net outcome of this change will be more positive for everyone. However, if you find yourself getting into an argument about any of these perceived benefits, return to yourself and your own emotions. Always return to you. You, and your need to express the best of you, is the real burning platform.

HONOR HIS FEARS. Allow him the opportunity to share what is impor-tant to him. Stay curious, and ask questions to get to the heart of his concerns. When you hear them, don't immediately refute them. Just let him air them. This will not only help him feel heard, it will help you devise a better strategy—if you know his true fears, you will know his true needs, and so you'll know better how to maneuver the situation so that these needs can be met.

BE READY TO ANSWER QUESTIONS. He will want to know things like: Will you be working longer hours? Will you be away a lot? How will this impact our time together? How will it impact our kids? Will it dis-rupt their schedule? How will we manage the finances? Have realistic answers ready.

How Do We Divide and Conquer?

In an interesting, yet hardly surprising survey of 5,848 men and 10,293 women conducted by MSNBC, respondents were asked if the chores in their households were performed by just one person or if they were shared. The results reveal that 74 percent of men said the chores were shared, compared to only 51 percent of women.

So apparently, despite living under the same roof, you and your spouse see things just a tad differently from one another. If you're feeling that you're doing more than your fair share, your spouse, as the survey shows, may not see it that way.

I'm not necessarily saying that one of you is right and the other wrong, but before you dive in to redress the balance, know that he may not be seeing the imbalance as quite as extreme as you do—if he even sees one at all.

Here are a few things you can do to open the lines of communication and, hopefully, arrive at ways to tilt the scales:

AS EVER, SET THE STAGE: Set a time to meet with your spouse to talk about your household responsibilities. You'll need twenty minutes max. Pick a spot where you can write. You do *not* need to come prepared with a list of everything that you do and everything he *doesn't* do. Instead, brainstorm all of the chores that have to be done on a daily, weekly, monthly, and yearly basis. Write them all down and group them by frequency.

SEARCH FOR STRENGTHS. Take turns volunteering for the chores that, though you may feel funny admitting it, you really enjoy doing. Don't assume that because you hate doing something, your partner does as well. (One of my favorite chores is washing dishes. I really love the feeling of the warm water. More than that, it is something in which I can feel an immediate sense of accomplishment. Sounds odd to say it out loud, but it is what it is.) Don't set yourself up for disappointment by thinking the tasks will end up evenly split. At this stage, just focus on selecting ones that you know are strengthening. If your kids are old enough, include them in the process. When your kids see you working hard to care for the home, they will be more inclined to pitch in.

SUBCONTRACT WHERE YOU CAN. Now, what do you do with all the chores on the list that fit no one's strengths? Can you subcontract any of them out? Have someone come to clean the house twice a month? Have a landscaper mow the yard one a month? Have an accountant keep your receipts? Obviously, your finances might not allow you to subcontract everything, but before you dismiss it as too expensive, remember that you might be able to generate more income with the time and the stress you save from paying someone else to do it. Even if the net financial gain is zero, the psychic gain might still make it worthwhile.

LIGHTEN UP THE LEFTOVERS. Inevitably, even after subcontracting, you'll have some leftover tasks that are weakening to both of you. Some tasks are definitely less attractive than others (cleaning the bathroom usually tops the list). Get creative on how you can accomplish them. Why not clean the bathroom together? Or split the duties in half and trade tasks the following month. How about creating an incentive program and have a prize for the person who gets the most points in the month? Twenty points for dog-doo pick up and five points for stove cleaning? Whatever you decide, make it about creating togetherness and make it fun.

SET UP A STANDING MEETING. Sitting down at least once a month with your spouse and kids to review how your plan is working is critical to keeping this plan alive. A meeting may sound too formal—it's just dust, after all—but this step is about accountability. This is a way of demonstrating to one another that you respect one another's time and effort.

AIM FOR . . . GOOD ENOUGH. Learn to live with a little disorder. If a pile of laundry, an overgrown yard, or a few dirty windows is the price that you have to pay for the strong-moment payoff of an afternoon skate with your family, or dinner and a movie with each other, so be it.

TACTICS FOR STRONGER KIDS

Children require guidance and sympathy
far more than instruction.

—ANNE SULLIVAN (1866–1936), American educator

○ **Should I Stay Home to Care for My Kids?**

○ **What Do I Do if Motherhood Weakens Me?**

○ **How Old Will My Kids Be When I Start to See
Their Strengths Emerge?**

○ **As A Parent, How Much of My Kid's Personality Can I Affect?**

○ **What Happens if the Teachers Insist on Focusing
on My Kid's Weaknesses?**

○ **What Can I Do to Help My Kids Develop Their Strengths?**

Should I Stay Home to Care for My Kids?

There is a heap of data on whether the better choice is to stay at home with your kids or put them in daycare. Whatever your opinion on the matter, you can find a study to back you up. My review of the research leads me to this conclusion: whether or not mothers work during their child's first three years has no ill effect on their child's social and intellectual development. You won't harm your kids by working.

Here's what I find far more interesting: If you are a working mother, do you know what your kids want? As I mentioned in the very beginning in the "Ten Myths," a nationally representative study of more than one thousand young people in the third through twelfth grades asked children: "If you were granted one wish that would change the way that your mother's/your father's work affects your life, what would that wish be?" In a parallel study, more than six hundred employed mothers and fathers were asked to guess what their children would wish. Here's what they found: "Most parents (56%) guessed that their children would wish for more time with them. But 'more time' was not at the top of children's wish list. Only 10% of children made that wish about their mothers and 15.5% made that wish about their fathers. Most children wished that their mothers (34%) and their fathers (27.5%) would be less stressed and tired."[1]

Your kids don't want more of your time; they want more of your happiness.

So, the best question to ask yourself is not "Should I work or stay home?" but rather "How do I raise strong kids while remaining happy and fulfilled?" We've dealt with the second part of the question throughout the book. We'll touch on the first part in the questions that follow.

What Do I Do If Motherhood Weakens Me?

You are not alone. I've never met a mother who loved being a mom the whole time. And this isn't just my opinion. Several well-executed studies surveying parents and nonparents reveal that kids don't make you happier.[2] Yes, I just wrote that. I know it sounds crazy because we have these cultural beliefs that children are the key to happiness and a healthy life, and, well, they're not. Parents report not only higher levels of stress than nonparents—as you would imagine, given how much of parenting feels like walking around with your heart outside your body—but also higher levels of boredom—another trip to Target, anyone? Fifteen more minutes of rolling that same plastic toy across the floor? Care to prepare yet another meal that your child will push around his plate and ultimately reject?

Don't misunderstand. I know you love your kids more than anything (as do I) and can't imagine life without them. But their gift to you isn't happiness. It is depth and meaning and purpose. And the research bears this out: parents report higher levels of purpose in their lives than adults without kids.

You become a parent not to feel happier, necessarily. You become a parent so you can love your kids and help them make their greatest contribution to the world.

If you are struggling to do that, approach mothering as you would any other area of responsibility in your life. You say, "I am starting to hate the mother I have become." My question is, "Who is the mother that you were?" When mothering was at its best, what were the activities that felt empowering and fulfilling? What were you doing at those times? Get specific and drill down into your experiences. It's not that your weaknesses lie in being a mother; it's that certain activities that you are currently engaged in are weakening.

So think back to what it looked like when being a mother "worked" for you. Try to pinpoint a few specific strong-moments and imbalance your life toward them—be deliberate about re-creating them, and then celebrate them when they happen. You may well find that you can tilt the role of mother so that it becomes more closely aligned to what strengthens you.

If, after searching for strong-moments and finding a few, you come to the conclusion that there's just not quite enough in mothering to fill your cup, look outside the home for other sources of strength. Part-time work, charity work, time with friends, physical exercise—any one of these may give you the energy you need.

To which you may say, "I'd love to, but I can't find the time. I have to be there for my kids."

To which I will reply, "You are serving no one, least of all your kids, if you do not take a stand for yourself. Your life *must* strengthen you, so that you can support those you love."

How Old Will My Kids Be When I Start to See Their Strengths Emerge?

While there are very few clear-cut "shoulds" in life, this may well be one of them: you should be on the lookout for your kids' strengths, because, by their second birthday, they have already shown you a library's worth of clues about what their strengths are.

One of the first sentences out of my daughter's mouth was, "That's a very pretty necklace." She was talking to Jane, and when this entire sentence came out of her three-year-old mouth, it's fair to say we were taken aback. First, she had barely put two words together until that moment; and second, in giving her mother a compliment, she clearly knew exactly what she was doing—more than simply being nice to her mom, she knew that she was spreading goodwill, and that at some point in the not-too-distant future, she would be able to use this goodwill to help her get something she wanted.

This is an incredibly sophisticated concept for a three-year-old to understand. We hadn't taught it to her. No one had taught it to her. Lilia was born with an innate understanding of the concept of recip-rocal altruism—namely, "I do something nice to you, and sooner or later you will do something nice for me." This isn't a second child thing, nor is it a girl thing. It is a Lilia thing (my guess for her Lead Role is Influencer).

I first noticed this "Lilia thing" as I walked with her one morning down the hallway leading from the assembly hall to her classroom. What should have taken three minutes took twenty as, every few yards, she was accosted by a shout, a squeal, and then some kind of smooch-lift-up-hug from one of the fourth, fifth, or sixth graders. At the time Lilia was barely three and had been at the school for precisely two months. Somehow during those two months she had managed to inveigle her way into the affections of students who shouldn't even have known she existed.

I'd call that a strength—or at least the beginnings of a strength, or a natural talent, if you will—and we saw it at age three.

The same will be true of your kids. Very soon after they are born, their behavior will take on repeating patterns, and with each passing month, as they interact with the world, as they acquire language, these patterns will become more robust and more predictable.

Look for the patterns from their very first moments—keep a journal of your insights and discoveries about each child—and you will give your child a most precious gift: your understanding.

As a Parent, How Much of My Kid's Personality Can I Affect?

Dear Marcus,

My child is ten years old, and I find myself butting heads with her all the time. She is so argumentative. When she doesn't clean up her room, I tell her to go back up and put everything away, but it always ends up in this big fight with her giving one excuse after another about why it's not her fault that her room's untidy. If I didn't just call a halt to it, and send her back up to her room, I swear she would keep arguing the whole night long. I end up just wanting to rip my hair out. It's really hurting our relationship. Is she always going to be this way? What can I do to stop her fighting and arguing all the time?

Dear X,

Initially this isn't going to be much consolation to you, but you can't stop her fighting and arguing. It's who she is. It might be annoying and challenging for you, as her mom, but it's one of her natural talents. You didn't give it to her, and you can't take it from her. All you can do—all any parent can do with her child—is help the child to channel her strengths in a productive way.

To give you a little background on this, what you need to remember is that you, the parent, do not significantly affect your child's personality. You can affect her values; you can affect her education; you can affect what new skills she is exposed to; you can even affect how comfortable she becomes with the peaks and valleys of her personality. But you don't create her personality at all.

Many of us think that there is a significant nature/nurture debate in our society—you know, the one about "Did I make my kid competitive because I put her on so many sports teams when she was young, or was she just born competitive?"—and we like to think that this debate is one of those profound unknowables, a metaphysical question that we can discuss long into the night but never answer.

The truth is that this debate was settled decisively more than a decade ago. And it was settled by a careful study of the personalities of identical twins who were adopted by different families and raised apart, in different homes, by different parents. To answer the nature/nurture question, all you have to do is find out whether the personalities of the twins are more like the parents who raised them or more like the parents who conceived them. And the answer to that question is always the same: the personalities of the twins resemble significantly the personalities of the parents who conceived them, and do not resemble at all the parents who raised them.[3]

This doesn't mean that you have no influence over how your kids behave. It simply means that each child is blessed with a unique pattern of traits and talents, and that you, the parent, have to try to mold and shape these patterns so that they become useful. In my first book, I wrote that the world's best managers live by the mantra: "Don't try to put in what God left out. Try to draw out what God left in. That's hard enough."

This mantra applies equally to parents.

So before you get into yet another argument with your daughter, think through how you can engage her talent for arguing and shape it so that it helps her rather than hurts her.

Not knowing your daughter, here are a few suggestions:

STOP BLAMING YOURSELF FOR HER BEHAVIOR. From your note, I'm not sure that you are blaming yourself, but if you are, please stop. There's nothing you did when she was a baby, there's no parenting slip up you made. If you need convincing of this, imagine that she was a complete pushover and didn't have either the appetite or the ability to argue at all. Now, try imagining what you would have to teach her in order to turn her into an arguing phenom; imagine all of the comeback phrases you'd have to school her in, and the instantaneous concocting of one excuse after another, the unbreakable desire to win the argument, and even the righteous indignation at being wronged. You couldn't do it. You couldn't even come close.

ASK HER TO DESCRIBE HER STRENGTHS TO YOU. Before you launch into a conversation about her combativeness, talk to her about her strengths. It might not work for you to try to cram this into one conversation, so be prepared to spread it out. But however you have it, the point is to get her talking about her strengths.

TELL HER THAT HER STRENGTHS ARE THOSE ACTIVITIES THAT MAKE HER FEEL STRONG. Many kids confuse "strength" with "performance." Schools make this mistake all the time, so be prepared to talk her through the idea that the two are different. We've tried this in a number of schools, and we find that the kids understand the distinction immediately—not surprising, really, given that most kids have a few subjects at school at which they do quite well, but which bore them to tears.

Your biggest challenge will be persuading your daughter that she is in fact the best judge of her strengths. After all, the most effective lesson schools teach is the idea that "you, the child, are not the authority on you—we are. We grade you, we rate you, we correct you, we know the right answer and your job is to learn what that answer is."

You are going to have to reeducate your daughter and show her that, when it comes to her strengths, *she* has the right answer. Ask her questions like, "When was the last time that a day just flew by? What were you doing?" Or "Was there any part of your day you looked forward to yesterday? What was it?" And then tell her that what she is talking about are her true strengths.

IF SHE DOESN'T BRING IT UP HERSELF, TELL HER THAT YOU THINK ONE HER STRENGTHS IS TO DEBATE. Affirm for her that this is a very useful strength to possess, and that she seems to have a great dollop of it. Talk to her about how and where this strength will prove useful, such as standing up for her friends or getting more information from one of her teachers. Tell her about some famous people who have also possessed this strength and how they used it to make a great contribution to the world.

LAST, TELL HER THAT STRENGTHS ARE POWERFUL AND THAT ONE OF HER CHALLENGES IS TO LEARN HOW TO CHANNEL THAT POWER. For example, explain to her that as a talented debater she could just go back and forth, back and forth, arguing forever; but that what the truly great debaters do is argue to achieve something; they argue to get an outcome. Tell her that the next time she is arguing about something, stop and think, *What outcome do I want?* and make sure to focus her argument toward that outcome. Or tell her that the great debaters always think about whom they are arguing with and tweak their argument so that it is most persuasive to this person (which in your case, will mean her thinking about you and how best to persuade you).

You might think this is too sophisticated to ask of your ten-year-old, but you'd be surprised. When you get your kids on the subject of their strengths, they are often light-years ahead of where their age says they should be, and sometimes light-years ahead of you. Just as Lilia is far more intelligent in the area of reciprocity than she should be, so your child will be alive to the possibilities and the innovations of effective arguing.

What Happens if the Teachers Insist on Focusing on My Kid's Weaknesses?

I do understand why many teachers believe that it is their responsibility to focus on improving your child's weak areas. They know that the child will struggle if she doesn't make the necessary grades, and so they want to do everything in their power to bolster her in those areas where she's struggling. It's all very well intended.

And yet, as you now know, while it may help your child survive—which, let's face it, is valuable—it will not help her excel. And excellence, helping her find her voice and make the greatest possible contribution to the world, must be your chief focus.

To help you get your child's teacher on board:

STATE YOUR BELIEF CLEARLY. Make this point clearly and often: "I want to push and stretch my child's learning, but I believe that my child's greatest opportunities for learning are in the areas where she already learns well."

DISCOVER TOGETHER. Ask her teacher, "Where is she at her best? Where does she learn the most?" Help the teacher by sharing the home activities that you've noticed make your child come to life.

LEVERAGE HER STRENGTHS. Ask, "Can we apply what she learns well to those areas she's struggling with?" She's incredible at math but struggles with writing? Ask that she write out her math questions using numbers instead of words. She's amazing at organizing, but struggles with long division? Can we help her envision long division in the same way she organizes her locker or her closet at home? She's great at painting but bad at vocabulary? After the class has read a book together, can we ask her to draw what the most difficult words mean, so that she can learn them, and, perhaps, so that other visual learners can learn them more easily as well?

Not every suggestion will be met with enthusiasm, but so long as you are clear and specific and positive, you will find that most teachers gravitate toward any idea that might help a child learn and grow.

What Can I Do to Help My Kids Develop Their Strengths?

Each child is blessed with a unique soul, whose voice is beautiful, perfect, and craves to be heard. As a parent you do not create your child; you create the conditions that allow her to express this beautiful, perfectly unique voice. How can you create these conditions?

WATCH HER. Spend one hour each week doing exactly what she wants to do. Don't judge what it is. Just ask her what she wants to spend an hour doing and do it with her. It could be something you approve of such as drawing a picture, or something you disapprove of such as playing a video game, but do it with her regardless. And watch her while she does it. What patterns are you seeing? Which part of the activity intrigues her? Which part does she look forward to the most?

HELP HER DEVELOP MASTERY. By all means give her the chance to try out new skills, and expose her to many opportunities, but channel her toward only a few. Mastery will serve her greatly as she grows up. It is a distinct feeling. To experience it, she must learn how to choose a particular skill and how to then set challenging goals for herself, goals that stretch her and keep her momentum going, but that are not so stretching that she never achieves them and becomes demoralized. She must learn how she learns, and how she practices, and what happens when she doesn't practice, and how she responds to this teacher or that teacher, and what it feels like to display her mastery for everyone to see. You will be able to tell her about each of these feelings, but only by deliberately trying to build mastery will she get to experience them herself.

TEACH HER HOW TO IDENTIFY HER OWN STRENGTHS. When your child is age nine or ten, you will be able to teach her the difference between her strengths—the activities that make her feel strong—and her performance. She will quickly grasp that, while you and her teachers and her coaches and her friends might be the best judge of her performance, she is the best judge of her strengths. Twice a year, ask her to carry a memo pad around with her for a week and keep track of which activities strengthened her, and which didn't, and then help her write three Strength Statements. Her first efforts might be quite generic, such as, "I like talking to my friends." You can help her become more detailed in her descriptions by asking her, "What is the verb? What are you actually *doing* with your friends? Are you just talking? Or are you laughing, or telling stories, or solving a problem?" You might think this is a little much for a nine-year-old, but you'd be surprised how wise she is about herself. Help her look closely at her own emotions, and she'll reveal to you such subtlety and detail.

GUIDE HER TOWARD MAKING A CONTRIBUTION. She has been blessed with beautiful strengths. But this beauty implies a responsibility: to express these strengths in the service of something greater than herself. This isn't a generic responsibility. It is specific to her. From a young age, you can ask her about how she is using the best of herself to help others. What are her friends relying on her for? What distinct contribution can she make to her class? What do her teammates on her sports teams look to her for? You will discover that she, like all children, is an instinctive individualizer; she knows that people differ in their talents and traits. By the age of three or four, she should be able to have detailed conversations with you about how she is different from her friends and what unique qualities she brings to her little world. As she grows up, these conversations will become increasingly vivid. Use them to guide her toward making a deliberate and distinctive contribution to others.

TEACH HER HOW TO USE HER STRENGTHS TO COPE WITH HER WEAKNESSES AND HER SETBACKS. The world will keep pulling your child toward who she is not. It will teach her that the best way to solve problems is to focus on them. It will show her how much there is to fear in the world. You can provide the countervailing influence in her life. You can teach her how to use her strengths to overpower, or make irrelevant her weaknesses. You can show her that focusing on what "working" looks like is a far more effective way to solve problems. You can introduce her to the idea that, while there is much to fear in the world, there is so much more to hope for.

BE HER ROLE MODEL. You don't have to be perfect—she wouldn't believe you even if you pretended to be. Instead, be a seeker. Show her that you too have a beautiful and unique voice that is asking to be heard, and, just like her, you are searching for how best to volunteer this voice to others. Tell her what your Lead Role is. Share your Strength Statements with her. Show her how your strengths saved you when circumstances set you back. Let her join you on your own journey.

TACTICS FOR A STRONGER FUTURE

Life itself is the proper binge.

—JULIA CHILD (1912–2004), American chef

How Do I Stop Feeling Overwhelmed?

How Can I Bounce Back from Setbacks?

How Do I Make Decisions I Don't Regret?

How Do I Stop Feeling Overwhelmed?

You won't be able to take care of the people you love unless you take care of yourself. So, to stop feeling pulled in a million directions, try this sequence of steps:

CAPTURE IT. Take the "overwhelm" out of your head and put it on paper, where you can distance yourself from it a bit. Write down every task you can think of that you are worrying about.

CHUNK IT. Once you've done this, group your tasks and to-dos into larger chunks. You'll probably come up with your own, but to help you get started, try: family, kids, career, partner, health. Organizing your to-dos into chunks will help you see your world more clearly.

CHOOSE IT. Your feelings of being overwhelmed don't spring from having too much on your plate, but from having too little, too little of what strengthens you. The specific activities that strengthen you have been drowned out by everything else. So, look at your chunks and prioritize your to-dos based on what makes you feel strong. Which ones do you love? Which ones are you actually looking forward to? Make a plan to do these first, and to find a small way to celebrate them when you've done them. Cradling these activities will give you strength and resilience to get through everything else.

TAKE ACTION. Action is the antidote to feeling overwhelmed. Very often it is not the activities themselves that stress us out but our worrying about the activities. Just begin. Very often the simple action of beginning will alleviate the anxiety and stress that has accumulated.

FOCUS. Focus on the task at hand. Think about what you are doing rather than what you're not getting done. Worry and time have an inverse relationship. The more you have of one, the less you have of the other. Both are suspended when you simply focus on what is in front of you right now.

How Can I Bounce Back from Setbacks?

Although we use the phrase *bounce back*—I've used it a couple of times in the book—the truth is you don't actually bounce back. You *build* back. Recovering from any traumatic situation is an incremental, intentional process, and it takes time.

DON'T EXPECT TO BOUNCE RIGHT BACK. You'll be holding yourself up to an impossible standard.

KEEP MOVING. Sitting around the house waiting for the next shoe to drop is a recipe for, well, the shoe to drop. So find some small thing you can do with your time. Can you find projects around the house? Can you sign up for a course at a local college? Can you complete a professional qualification?

FIND SOMEONE TO HELP. Who can you help? Can you find a local non-profit that could benefit from your skills? Is there an elderly relative you haven't seen in a while who would love a little of your company? Try to find somebody—it doesn't really matter who—who will value what you bring.

RALLY AROUND YOUR CERTAINTIES. Which strong-moments are still possible in your life? Do everything in your power to re-create them this week, and celebrate them. And remember, *celebrate* doesn't just mean clap and cheer. It means give them your full attention. It means think of creative ways to build on these strong-moments. It means asking yourself, "Where could these lead me? What do these moments reveal about this best of me? Who could benefit from the best of me?"

USE YOUR CRISIS TO CLARIFY WHO YOU ARE AND WHAT IS IMPORTANT TO YOU. I'm not going to tell you to keep a positive attitude—that's Pollyanna, and unhelpful. But I will tell you that there is opportunity to be found in setback, and the opportunity is to become clearer about which aspects of yourself you can count on the most. When the winds aren't blowing, it's hard to separate strengths from weaknesses; it's hard to see what is uniquely powerful about you. But when the winds are blowing hard, your weaknesses lie flat, leaving only your strengths standing tall. The word *crisis* actually comes from the Greek word *krisis*, which means to decide. Setbacks can reveal the core of you; they can challenge you to face up to what matters to you, and so they afford you the rare opportunity to *decide* which path to take.

How Do I Make Decisions I Don't Regret?

Regret, though a powerful and debilitating feeling, doesn't exist in the present. It's only possible to feel regret when you are looking backward in time, after you've made your decision, after you've seen the outcome of your decision and, for some reason, you wish the outcome were different. In retrospect, you can regret—literally cry over—an *outcome*.

But you can never regret a decision. A decision exists in the present and concerns the future. And since you will never know in advance whether a decision is the right one—you can't see into the future—your most realistic goal is to try to make your decision with confidence. You can't control the outcome, but you can control how you think about and think through your decision.

The typical way to think through a decision is to analyze all the variables, make a list of pros and cons, and then see which list carries the day. Have you ever tried this? Whenever I did it, I found that, as I made my list, I deliberately skewed one list so that by the time I'd finished, my pros and cons wound up pointing to the decision I'd already made. And I knew it. I hadn't faked myself out. Which meant that I didn't end up any more confident in my decision.

The secret to confident decision-making doesn't lie in analysis and list-making. It lies in accessing the emotions that are going to make your decision for you anyway. To access these emotions and channel them—as opposed to being surprised by them later—always ask yourself these three questions before you make any major decision in life:

Which choice will enable me to experience more strong-moments in each aspect of my life?

Which choice will provide me the best opportunity to learn more in my areas of strength?

Which decision will allow me to make the greatest contribution in my areas of strength?

Each of these questions is about you and how you feel about you. Initially this might appear self-centered—shouldn't you be thinking about your family or your spouse?—but the reason to do it is because you want as much certainty as possible before you make your decision.

Of all the variables in your head right now—your family's needs, your future earning power, your potential work colleagues—you are most certain of your own feelings. Tease those feelings out, see in which direction they point, and you will make a decision based on *your* truth, as you know it. At some point in the future you may have cause to regret the outcome of the decision—who knows what the future holds—but you will always be able to look back and know you made your decision based on what you knew for certain about you. That is all you can do, and all you need to do.

14

BACK IN THE BOAT

You may have a fresh start at any moment,
because this thing we call "failure" is not
the falling down, but the staying down.

—MARY PICKFORD (1893–1979), American actress

Charlie's time in the hospital gave her the chance to reflect on the moments she wanted to create in her life.

She had some immediate matters to take care of. She finally had the conversation with Peter, not in quite the location she'd imagined—she was thinking a nice restaurant, not her hospital bed—but she had it. And Peter, having sorted through all the piles on her desk and having made some rather unpleasant discoveries about the state of their finances, finally agreed to hire a part-time bookkeeper.

But the more important choices concerned her future.

She thought about the moments when it felt like her life was "working" and she realized that, ironically, she had been most fulfilled when she was counseling her daughter's class after their friend's suicide. She had been a counselor before, of course, but always with potentially violent offenders. Mulling over it now, she realized that it was the violence, or rather the possibility of violence, that ruined the experience for her.

If she could stick to grief counseling, maybe she could be happy. And not just the counseling itself, but setting up the counseling programs. When she went with her daughter to the school right after the suicide, she was not impressed with the way support was provided to the students—a horde of counselors descended on the school for a few days and then left. Charlie knew that in the first week the kids were in shock and that they would need most help in the weeks and months following, after the deep sadness, the guilt, and the fear had finally settled in to do their worst.

Typical Charlie, she thought she could see a better way of doing it, a more systematic way that would provide students with longer-term support.

And that's what she's doing now, setting up grief counseling programs for high schools across the state.

In doesn't pay much yet, so she has taken a job at a local health club to help with some of the household expenses, but this decision is also part of her strong life plan. She used to be far fitter, a hiker, a camper, a frequent competitor in local sailing competitions.

"But I stopped," she told me. "What with the job and the stress and everything, I just didn't have the energy. The gym job gives me free membership, so now I get to work out, play tennis, and swim as often as I like. I really want to get that part of my life back."

How's it going?

"Well I've still got a ways to go with my tennis, but I'll tell you this," she grinned. "When my boat capsizes in a race, I can finally pull myself back in."

As with Charlie, so with you. Early in the research for this book, I met a woman who had it all. An American based in the UK, she had joined a young company whose groundbreaking technology lacked only the mechanism to generate revenue. As their head of marketing she had discovered a way to monetize the value of the technology, and the company's revenues had swelled into the billions. Hailed as that rarest of creatures, a visionary who can also turn her visions into reality, she had, after cashing in her stock options, found herself with more money than she would ever be able to spend in her lifetime. Along the way she had married a supportive husband, and together they had had three children, who, when I met her, were all under six.

So what does she do now, this woman who has everything, who can do anything, be anything she wants to be?

If she wished, both she and her husband could quit work forever, take the children to school, spend a couple of mornings reading to the kids in class or chairing a school committee, and then devote the rest of each day to their chosen charity, or community work, or simply hang together and do all the things that the rest of us say we would do with our spouse if work didn't get in the way, until it was time to pick up the kids, make a game of cooking dinner, eat together each night at the family table, and relax into the nightly ritual of bath time, reading, cuddling, and sleep.

But she doesn't do this. Instead, she has chosen to assume the presidency of one the fastest growing, highest risk, and highest profile companies in the world, with all of its attendant challenges, pressures, thrills, and time constraints.

Is hers the right choice? Only she can judge.

Even if everything works out seemingly perfectly for you, you will still face the reality that life is a series of choices only you can make. Setbacks will happen, plans will change, relationships can disappoint, your career will rarely pan out quite the way you planned.

Whatever you take away from this book, know that the secret to success and happiness lies in your ability to know yourself well enough to make strong choices without regret, no matter what life bestows on you, or throws at you.

Slow your judgments, accept what you feel is right for you, and trust that your "soul's code" contains within it all the wisdom you will ever need.

Quit your balancing act, and start intentionally imbalancing your days and weeks toward the strong-moments in each part of your life.

Your strongest life lies so close to you, familiar and startling, waiting to be found.

NOTES

Ten Myths

1. B. Stevenson and J. Wolfers, "The Paradox of Declining Female Happiness" Philadelphia: University of Pennsylvania, working paper, 2007.

2. Anke C Plagnol and Richard A. Easterlin "Aspirations, Attainments, and Satisfaction: Life Cycle Differences between American Women and Men," *Journal of Happiness Studies*, vol. 9 (2008): 601–19.

3. U.S. Department of Labor, Bureau of Labor Statistics, Employment and Earnings, 2007 Annual Averages and the Monthly Labor http://www.dol.gov/wb/stats/main.htm (November 9, 2008).

4. Ellen Galinsky, Kerstin Aumann, and James P. Bond, "Times are Changing: Gender and Generation at Work and at Home," Families and Work Institutes "The 2008 National Study of the Changing Workforce," 9.

5. Gallup Poll, "If you were taking a new job and had your choice of a boss would you prefer to work for a man or a woman?" (August 7–10, 2006) N=1,007 adults nationwide. MoE ± 3 (for all adults). http://www.pollingreport.com/work.htm (accessed November 23, 2008).

6. M. Mattingly and L. Sayer "Under Pressure: Gender Differences in the Relationship between Free Time and Feeling Rushed," *Journal of Marriage and Family*, vol. 68 (2006): 205–21.

7. R.J. Evenson and R. Simon "Clarifying the Relationship Between Parenthood and Depression," *Journal of Health and Social Behavior*, vol. 46 (2005): 341–58.

8. J. Coleman and S. Coontz, eds. "What Do Children Want from their Working Parents? *Unconventional Wisdom: A Survey of Research and Clinical Findings.* Prepared for the Council on Contemporary Families' Tenth Anniversary Conference at the University of Chicago. http://www.contemporaryfamilies.org/subtemplate.php?t=briefingPapers&ext=unconventionalwisdom(accessed December 4, 2008).

9. R. Moroney "Men and Women Are Equally Bad at Multitasking," (March 7, 2007, *Wall Street Journal* http://blogs.wsj.com/informedreader/2007/03/07/men-and-women-are-equally-bad-at-multitasking/ (accessed January 13, 2009);

Hewlett Packard, "Abuse of technology can reduce UK workers intelligence," http://www.scribd. com /doc/6910385/Abuse-of-technology-can-reduce-UK-workers-intelligence (accessed January 13, 2009).

10. "Exactly how much housework does a husband create?" (University of Michigan News Service, April 3, 2008) http://www.ns.umich.edu/htdocs/releases/story.php?id=6452 (accessed January 28, 2009).

Chapter 1: One Workshop, One Show, One Hundred Thousand Questions

1. Marcus Buckingham, *Now, Discover Your Strengths* (New York: Free Press, 2001); *Go Put Your Strengths to Work* (New York: Free Press, 2007); *The Truth About You* (Nashville: Thomas Nelson, 2008).

Chapter 2: The Female Paradox

1. National Center for Education Statistics, Projections of Education Statistics to 2015. http://nces.ed.gov/pubsearch/pubsinfo.asp?pubid=2006084.

2. 2006 American Community Survey http://factfinder.census.gov.

3. June Ellenoff O'Neil, "The Gender Gap in Wages, Circa 2000." *American Economic Review*, vol. 93, no. 2 (2003): 309–13

4. B. Stevenson and J. Wolfers, "The Paradox of Declining Female Happiness" Philadelphia: University of Pennsylvania, working paper, 2007.

5. James Allan Davis and Tom W. Smith, *General Social Surveys, 1972–2006*, Principal Investigator, James A. Davis; Director and Co-Principal Investigator, Tom W. Smith; Co-Principal Investigator, Peter V. Marsden; Sponsored by National Science Foundation. NORC ed. Chicago: National Opinion Research Center [producer]; Storrs, CT: The Roper Center for Public Opinion Research, University of Connecticut [distributor], 2007. The Average Happiness Index values were calculated by assigning values of one (1) to all respondents who indicated they were "not too happy," values of two (2) to all responses of "pretty happy," and values of three (3) to responses of "very happy," and then averaging the results for a given year and sex.

6. Anke C Plagnol and Richard A. Easterlin "Aspirations, Attainments, and Satisfaction: Life Cycle Differences between American Women and Men," *Journal of Happiness Studies*, vol. 9 (2008): 601–19.

7. R. A. Easterlin, "Aspirations, Attainments, and Satisfaction: Life Cycle Differences Between American Women and Men," *Journal of Happiness Studies*, vol.9, no. 4 (2008): 612. Reprinted with permission from R. A. Easterlin.

8. M. Mattingly and L. Sayer "Under Pressure: Gender Differences in the Relationship between Free Time and Feeling Rushed," *Journal of Marriage and Family*, vol. 68 (2006): 205–21.

9. World Health Organization, "The Global Burden of Disease," Part 4 (2004), 46.

Chapter 3: Of Choice and Men

1. Gallup Poll, August 13–16, 2007, N=1,019 adults nationwide, http://www.pollingreport.com/work.htm (accessed February 5, 2009).

2. S. Coontz, "Motherhood Stalls When Women Can't Work. Council on Contemporary Families," 2007.

3. Douglas J. Besharov, "Poverty Update: The Long-Term Story Behind the New Numbers." American Enterprise Institute for Public Policy Research, September 2007, www.aei.org/docLib/20070927_3122220-OTIBesharov_g.pdf (accessed July 23, 2009).

4. Barry Shwartz, *Paradox of Choice* (New York: Harper Perennial, 2004).

5. Families and Living Arrangements, http://www.census.gov/Press-Release/www/releases/archives/families_households/009842.html (accessed 2006).

6. Bureau of Labor Statistics, American Time Use Survey Summary—2007 Results, November 12, 2008, www.bls.gov/news/release.auts.nr0.htm (accessed December 4, 2008).

7. Suzanne M. Bianchi, John P. Robinson, and Melissa A. Milkie. *Changing Rhythms of American Family Life*, Rose Series in Sociology, (New York: Russell Sage Foundation Publications, 2006).

8. Kimberley, Fisher, Muriel Egerton, Jonathan I. Gershuny, and John P. Robinson, Gender convergence in the American Heritage Time Use Study (AHTUS), Social Indicators Research (2006).

9. "Exactly how much housework does a husband create?" (University of Michigan News Service, April 3, 2008) http://www.ns.umich.edu/htdocs/releases/story.php?id=6452 (accessed January 28, 2009).

10. Jonathan I.Gershuny, Michael Bittman, and John Brice, "Exit, Voice and Suffering: Do Couples Adapt to Changing Employment Patterns?" *Journal of Marriage and Family*, vol. 67 (2005): 656–65.

11. Unpublished data from Survey of Income and Program Participation

12. Tallese D. Johnson, "Maternity Leave and Unemployment Patterns of First-Time Mothers: 1961–2003," United States Census Bureau, Issued February 2008 (http://www.census.gov/prod/2008pubs/p70-113.pdf accessed July 27, 2009).

13. Susan C. Eaton, "If You Can Use Them: Flexible Policies, Organizational Commitment and Perceived Performance," *Industrial Relations*, Vol 42, no. 2 (2003): 145–67.

14. Michael Burda, Daniel S. Hamermesh, Philippe Weil, "Total Work, Gender and Social Norms," NBER Working Papers 13000, National Bureau of Economic Research, Inc. (2007).

15. W. Kirn, "The Autumn of the Multitaskers," *The Atlantic* (November, 2007), http://www.theatlantic.com/doc/200711/multitasking (accessed January 10, 2009).

16. Hewlett Packard, "Abuse of Technology Can Reduce UK Workers Intelligence," (April 22, 2005), http://www.scribd.com/doc/6910385/Abuse-of-technology-can-reduce-UK-workers-intelligence (accessed January 13, 2009).

Chapter 9: Strive for Imbalance

1. Here I am indebted to the work of David Cooperrider, whose seminal article introducing the concept of Appreciative Inquiry, titled "Appreciative Inquiry in Organizational Life" can be found in *Research in Organizational Change and Development*, vol. 1 (Greenwich: JAI Press): 129–69.

2. S. L. Murray, J. G. Holmes, D. Dolderman, and D. W. Griffin, "What the Motivated Mind Sees: Comparing Friends' Perspectives to Married Partners' Views of Each Other," *Journal of Experimental Social Psychology*, vol. 36 (2000): 600–20.

Chapter 11: Tactics for Stronger Relationships

1. Gary Chapman, *The Five Love Languages: How to Express Heartfelt Commitment to Your Mate* (Northfield, IL: Northfield Publishing, 1995).

Chapter 12: Tactics for Stronger Kids

1. J. Coleman and S. Coontz, eds. "What Do Children Want from their Working Parents? *Unconventional Wisdom: A Survey of Research and Clinical Findings.* Prepared for the Council on Contemporary Families' Tenth Anniversary Conference at the University of Chicago. http://www.contemporaryfamilies.org/subtemplate.php?t=briefingPapers&ext=unconventionalwisdom(accessed December 4, 2008).

2. R. J. Evenson and R. Simon, "Clarifying the Relationship Between Parenthood and Depression," *Journal of Health and Social Behavior*, vol. 46 (2005): 341–58.

3. Judith Rich Harris, *No Two Alike: Human Nature and Human Individuality*, (New York: W. W. Norton and Company), 2006.

ABOUT THE AUTHOR

Marcus Buckingham, founder of The Marcus Buckingham Company, is a best-selling author with more than 3.7 million copies of his landmark bestsellers in print. He has been profiled in the *New York Times*, *Fortune*, *Fast Company*, *Harvard Business Review*, and *USA Today*.

Marcus spent nearly two decades at the Gallup Organization pioneering research into personal strengths and has developed strengths-based business solutions for some of the world's most recognizable brands, such as Best Buy, Disney, and Toyota.

Buckingham graduated from Cambridge University in 1987 with a master's degree in Social and Political Science. He is a member of the Secretary of State's Advisory Committee on Leadership and Management. He lives with his wife and two children in Los Angeles.

ACKNOWLEDGMENTS

This book grew out of an attempt to reply to the hundreds of thousands of posts we received on Oprah.com, so first off I need to thank everyone at Harpo who crafted the show and created the platform for such widespread and intense conversation; in particular Katy Davis and Gina Sprehe at the Oprah Winfrey Show, and Marietta Hurwitz and Stephanie Snipes at Oprah.com.

Tim Geary carved the first words of this book and gained us traction when we needed it most. Tracy Hutton was my constant collaborator, questioner, and researcher, who always managed to discover the nugget hidden in the thicket of peer-reviewed articles and journals.

Massive thanks to my team at TMBC, Elvie Moore, Stephanie Daniels and Jessica Lee; Jaqai Mickelsen for his design sense and sensibility; Courtney McCashland for her question-writing genius; and Charlotte Jordan for her empathy, constancy and wisdom.

To the entire Thomas Nelson team, thank you for your faith in this project. Thank you Jeff Loper for your patience and conscientiousness; to Heather Adams for your class; to Brian Hampton for your wise, guiding hand; and to my editor, Bryan Norman, for being such a thoughtful, respectful yet challenging partner.

To my agent at WME, Jennifer Rudolf Walsh, my undying admiration.

To my family, thank you for your long-suffering patience for most of last year.

And, of course, to all those who consented to be interviewed for the book, thank you for your candor, your vulnerability, and your passion.

Chances are you know other women who are struggling to find the life that is meant for them. Explore the principles of *Find Your Strongest Life* with friends, co-workers, a reading group or an organization with which you are involved. The *Find Your Strongest Life* Discussion Series comprises eight sessions to guide participants in achieving a stronger life at home and work.

The Discussion Series includes:

» **Video Introduction** from Marcus Buckingham.

» **Leader's Guide** that provides direction on leading a small discussion series and offers additional exercises to stimulate participant engagement.

» **Participant's Guide** that contains key book passages and questions to spur group discussion and personal reflection, and exercises to help women understand, evaluate, and apply the book's material.

» **Eight Strong Life Plans** from which women can choose those most applicable to their own lives. Each plan offers clear, practical steps for obtaining a stronger, happier, more successful life.

» **Collateral Kit** offering flyers and postcards to help you spread the word about your discussion series and encourage others to join you in the *Find Your Strongest Life* journey.